In the
Biblical
Preacher's
Workshop

# In the Biblical Preacher's Workshop

Dwight E. Stevenson

Abingdon Press

NASHVILLE AND NEW YORK

IN THE BIBLICAL PREACHER'S WORKSHOP

*Copyright © 1967 by Abingdon Press*

*ISBN 0-687-19005-3*

*Library of Congress Catalog Card Number: 67-14988*

SET UP, PRINTED, AND BOUND BY THE
PARTHENON PRESS, AT NASHVILLE,
TENNESSEE, UNITED STATES OF AMERICA

To my mother
**Mabel Eshelman Stevenson**
whose love of the Bible cradled me
in the love of God from my
infant years and inspires me
until this present hour

Gratis

84186

# Preface

The purpose of this book is twofold: (1) to help bridge the
gap between the exegetical and homiletical treatment of the
Bible, i.e., to get scholarship and preaching back together
following a long estrangement; (2) to give practical guidance
in the handling of scripture passages of intermediate length
(there is only one chapter on short texts).

The method of the book is "tell and show," a kind of lecture-
demonstration in book form. It does not aim at the multiplication of sermon ideas or the sprouting of numerous "sermon
starters." Rather it aims to lay out a way of working which will
enable a minister to make an increasingly creative use of the
Bible in his own preaching. The important thing about the
book is process. This process is both described and demonstrated. The description is given in Part I, entitled "Design";
the demonstration, in Part II, labeled "Production."

Procedures outlined have been laboratory tested. Over a
period of several years I have evolved them in interaction with
my students while together we have sought a way of learning
how to make a creative approach to the Bible as the genuine
source of pulpit proclamation. The minister who will do his
"homework," which requires him to be a student in the first

7

part of his preparation for each sermon, will find a new dimension of authority and power growing within his preaching. I offer the book with confidence that its method will work because I have seen it work.

One hope I have in presenting the book is to bring to my earlier students some of the maturing insights of later years which were denied them at the time but to which they contributed greatly in the period of this book's gestation. I salute all my students from 1947 until the present: "Thank you for what you have taught me."

I am grateful also to Martha Obenshain, faculty secretary, who in typing the manuscript and in helping with proofreading applied her own high standards of professional excellence. My wife, De Loris, as is usual when I am working on a book, has helped by her encouragement and her critical reading of manuscript and printer's proofs.

DWIGHT E. STEVENSON

Lexington Theological Seminary
Lexington, Kentucky

# Contents

**Part I. DESIGN**

Introduction: The Return to the Bible                          13

1. The Inherent Purpose of the Bible                           17
2. The Bible and the Word of God                               34
3. Some Presuppositions in Biblical Interpretation             46
4. The Minister as a Biblical Student                          58
5. The Minister as a Biblical Preacher                         71

**Part II. PRODUCTION**

6. Preaching on a Biblical Personality                         91
7. Preaching on a Parable                                     107
8. Preaching on a Miracle                                     126
9. Preaching on a Short Text                                  146
10. Preaching on a Psalm                                      159
11. Preaching on a Perplexing Passage                         178
12. Preaching on a Major Biblical Theme                       194

Epilogue: Servant of the Word                                 211

Index of Scripture                                            215
Index of Names and Subjects                                   218

# Part I

# DESIGN

# Introduction
## The Return to the Bible

One of my students recently told this story: A young man came to an older minister greatly perturbed. "Last Sunday," he said, "I preached my first sermon, and when I finished I began to realize that I had told everything I know. But I have to preach next Sunday. What am I going to say? I thought maybe you could give me a book or something to help me out."

The older minister handed him a book. "Try this," he said. "I think you will find it helpful." The young man took the book and departed, greatly relieved. It was a Bible.

The following Monday he reappeared, jubilant. "It was great," he exulted in reporting the experience of preaching from the Bible, "simply great! But what am I going to do next Sunday?"

This story serves as a chiding caricature of topical preaching at its worst. Topical preaching is a function of the institutional church, rooted in the idealism of the preacher and taking its values from what one philosopher has called "America's spiritual culture." To the extent that this kind of preaching uses the Bible at all, it does so to exploit or devour it and not to listen to it, let alone to stand under it and be guided by it.

Topical preaching is dying. It is dying both because of its own sterility and because of the clash of values within contemporary culture. In consequence, by a kind of unarticulated desperation, ministers are being driven to the Bible. This return to biblical preaching is nowhere more entertainingly depicted than by Yale's late Halford E. Luccock in his homiletical classic, *In the Minister's Workshop*. Writing of the crop of preachers who graduated from seminary about 1910 he said:

In those days quite a number of young Apolloses, on graduating, having become men, put away such childish things as texts and Bible stories. In the pulpit they lived amid the immensities and starry galaxies. But after a while, when their little long-suffering congregations had heard the sermon on "The March of Progress" (for progress was marching in those days) and the one on "Science and Religion" and the one on "Pragmatism" (for pragmatism was going big then), like the prodigal son, they began to be in want. Then they came to themselves and said, "In my father's Book are texts enough and to spare." And they said, "I will arise and go to the Bible." [1]

So much for the return of the prodigal. This return has not been without a rather smug witness who has not been above saying, "I told you so." I refer to the biblically oriented elder brother who never deserted textual preaching. He stayed comfortably at home in his father's book. And while the returning prodigal is shamefacedly confessing his recent disgrace, his elder brother has been wanting to say to his father, "Lo, these many years have I served you, and I never preached a topical sermon; yet you never gave me a big church with a prominent pulpit that I might make merry with my friends."

The poverty and unbiblical character of topical preaching are now evident almost everywhere to almost everybody. And the prodigals are flocking home by the hundreds. But the

[1] (Apex ed.; Nashville: Abingdon Press, 1944) , p. 149.

poverty and unbiblical character of much textual preaching are not so obvious. It has all the outward marks of fidelity. Yet it may be just as false.

The truth of the matter is that God has not one but two rebellious sons—one who went to a far country and one who stayed at home with his far country inside him. Both need to come to themselves and arise and go to their father. Jesus in his parable completed the story of the prodigal, but he left the story of the elder brother unfinished. I suspect that he did this because he was talking to a whole crowd of elder brothers. Only they could finish the story by their own response to this challenge.

The point is this: We may have been doing so-called biblical preaching all our lives, or we may have returned recently, but we may be missing the central thrust and reigning spirit of the Bible. All our words when taken in sum may add up to nothing better than "Lord, Lord." For all our knowledge of the words of scripture, we may be missing the Word with a capital W. In the pride of our text-girded and scripture-laden sermons we may say, "Lord, did we not prophesy in your name, and cast out demons in your name, and do many mighty works in your name?" But the Lord may answer, "I never knew you; depart from me, you evildoers" (Matt. 7:21-23).

For the word of God is alive and active. It cuts more keenly than any two-edged sword, piercing as far as the place where life and spirit, joints and marrow, divide. It sifts the purposes and thoughts of the heart. There is nothing in creation that can hide from him; everything lies naked and exposed to the eyes of the One with whom we have to reckon." (Heb. 4:12-13 NEB.)

No one is as much in danger of being electrocuted as an electrician whose trade compels him to work with high-tension

15

lines. And no Christian is as much in danger of becoming a castaway as a minister who wrongly handles the word of truth. Both trades need a warning sign in large red letters, "Danger! High Voltage!"

This leads us, it seems to me, to only one conclusion: We are servants of the Word and not its masters, as our ministerial pride would lead us at times to suppose. Not only are we servants of the Word; as things now stand, we are unprofitable servants. A realization of this fact will drive us, to the extent that it becomes a torment, to go to the Bible with a new urgency. Certain questions will goad us: In relation to the Bible, what *is* the Word of God? Is the Word of God identical with the words of scripture? If not, what is the relation between the Word and these words?

To be confronted by these questions and others like them is to be driven to some hard thinking in biblical theology and to some real wrestling with our presuppositions and principles of biblical interpretation. Such questioning will necessitate a recovery of the disciplines of hermeneutics and a new engagement with the homiletics of a new approach to biblical preaching.

Here the pulpit giants of past generations cannot greatly help us. To have passed through the revelations of modern biblical scholarship and then to design our preaching on nineteenth-century models which do not take these insights into account is to betray our trust. For the modern pulpit there is consequently no *return* to the Bible—no restoration of biblical preaching as our grandfathers knew it. The direction is not backward but forward—along new trails, freshly blazed, to new frontiers not occupied before. In such pioneering we inch our way forward amid uncertainty and peril. Nevertheless, we must advance. For the greater peril is to remain where we are, on quaking ground.

# 1

## The Inherent Purpose of the Bible

The relation of the Bible to the Word of God is not as simple as one might suppose. Consider two opposite views of the matter. The first is that of John Burgon, a nineteenth-century Oxonian who took the position that the Word of God is identical with the words of the Bible:

> The Bible is none other than the voice of Him that sitteth upon the throne. Every book of it, every chapter of it, every letter of it, is the direct utterance of the Most High. The Bible is none other than the Word of God, not some part of it more, some part of it less, but all alike the utterance of Him who sitteth upon the throne, faultless, unerring, supreme.[1]

Over against such a view, place that of a twentieth-century biblical scholar, Edwin Cyril Blackman. Expressing the thought of many colleagues he says, "It is agreed that there is a Word from God. We are also agreed that this Word is mediated by the Bible but is not coextensive with, or identifiable with, the books of the Bible." [2]

---

[1] Quoted in J. Estlin Carpenter, *The Bible in the Nineteenth Century* (London: Longmans, Green, and Co., 1903), p. 7.

[2] *Biblical Interpretation* (Philadelphia: Westminster Press, 1959), pp. 18-19.

To which of these views do you hold? Or do you perhaps occupy a position somewhere between the two extremes, or even to the left of both? Before you can preach from the Bible you should settle the question of the relation of scripture to the Word of God. To be fuzzy at this point is to confuse the preaching ministry from start to finish. Nevertheless, it is evident that for many biblical preachers this remains an unasked —not to say an unanswered—question. In this chapter and the next we must ask it and attempt an answer.

## Why the Bible?

Why should there be a Word of God in the first place? Why— to what purpose—the Bible at all? This question is not often asked—at least, not explicitly. But implicitly it is always asked and answered in some way by the biblical reader. He assumes a certain purpose for the Bible from the standpoint which he occupies as he reads it or listens to expositions on it. His assumptions may be sound or they may be flimsy, but he will have them; what he is able to get from the Bible will be limited by them.

It is wise to take these assumptions into account. The preacher will have his own assumptions, perhaps differing from those of other preachers and from the views of his congregation. Moreover, members of the congregation will differ among themselves in these matters. There is one Bible, but in the reading or hearing, its single light may be refracted by the varying or conflicting mind-set of those who read and those who hear, so that the unity of the original source is broken—by human preconceptions—into jarring contradictions. "Why the Bible?" is a question that must be faced at the beginning of any solid program of biblical preaching.

18

## Seven Inadequate Answers

Consider seven different answers "alive and kicking" in the contemporary church. (1) *The Bible exists to tell us what to do.* It is a manual of behavior, particularly in the realm of morals and ritual. Or, to state the matter differently, the Bible is a law book containing the explicit commands of God. Certain churchmen of an earlier century distinguished between the "positive" and "moral" commands of the Bible. By "positive" they meant such commands as were contained in the words of Jesus instituting the Lord's Supper, "This do in remembrance of me," or giving the Great Commission, "Go, make disciples . . . baptizing them in the name of the Father, and of the Son, and of the Holy Spirit." By "moral" commands they meant such rules as "Thou shalt not bear false witness" and "Thou shalt love thy neighbor as thyself." These commands were to be obeyed simply, unquestioningly, just as an army private obeys his commanding officer. The commands of God, transmitted through the Bible, are usually conceived in very specific, literalistic terms.

This answer may be objected to on several grounds. Theologically, it turns the whole Bible into a burden of law. It makes God into a stern lawgiver, policeman, and judge, and leaves no room for God the compassionate Redeemer. It makes no provision for gospel. Psychologically, it condemns the believer to self-righteousness, if he remains blameless before the law; or to despair, if he falls short of its high requirements. Historically it is inaccurate. While the Bible does contain commandments and laws, the whole of it is not a law book. It also contains prayers, poems, allegories and parables, prophetic oracles, historical chronicles, and many other literary forms which can never be reduced to explicit ritual or moral commands. Practically, it is indefensible because it condemns to ambiguity great tracts of scripture from which one supposedly should

19

extract clear and sufficient light upon daily problems of human behavior and conduct. What rules, for example, can one derive from the story of Jephthah's sacrifice of his daughter in fulfillment of his vow as related in Judges, chapter 11? Is this for or against human sacrifice? Are we supposed to admire Jephthah or condemn him, repudiate his example or emulate it?

Take another example, this one documented by biographical fact. A young woman, who later became a celebrated religious leader in the Salvation Army, was contemplating marriage with a young man who was not a believer. Seeking guidance, she opened her Bible and read II Cor. 6:14 with its very specific direction, "Do not be mismated with unbelievers." As a result of consulting the Bible in this manner she refused the young man his suit and remained a spinster throughout the rest of her long life. One wonders what might have happened if she had chanced to open the Bible at I Cor. 7:14: "For the unbelieving husband is consecrated through his wife."

(2) *The Bible exists to supply "spiritual" information.* It reveals the facts about such esoteric matters as heaven and hell, and the map of the future. On these points the Bible lifts the veil of mystery and satisfies human curiosity. In particular, it makes the chief role of the Bible *predictive.* It removes our finite uncertainty about the future, whether it be the eschatological future of the individual or the historical future of the race. Of those holding such an assumption regarding the purpose of the Bible, a scholar of another century wrote:

As to the future, they feel themselves elevated upon the shoulders of both the lesser and the greater Prophets; and seeing, therefore, afar off, can tell you the very day, and give a shrewd guess as to the hour of the second Advent, and demonstrate the correctness of their views not only prophetically, but chronologically, arithmetically, hieroglyphically, pictorially, and almost geologically. To these persons there is nothing new or unlooked for, and . . . they wonder

20

at nothing, unless it be at the only mystery which they admit to be inexplicable—to wit, that everybody will not agree with them in their opinion.[3]

Some think of this predictive function of the Bible in more mundane terms. There are those who think they find the invention of the automobile and the airplane, the rise of Hitler, and the explosion of the A-bomb foretold there. (These "predictions" are conveniently read after the fact in most instances.)

Against such a view of the main function of the Bible there are two objections: (a) Practically, there is the record of human disagreement. How many times has the date for the predicted end of the world come and gone? If God had intended to give us this information through the Bible, it would appear that he would have left the words open to less ambiguous interpretation! (b) Theologically, there is the fact that man is finite. This means that he is time-bound, that only God knows the future. Anyone wanting an explicit word from the Bible itself warning against these predictions of the last day may find it: "But of that day and hour no one knows, not even the angels of heaven, nor the Son, but the Father only" (Matt. 24:36). It would seem that this should settle the matter; but such is the curious fascination of the predictive view of scripture for certain interpreters that this verse becomes invisible before their eyes. They simply fail to see it; or seeing it, refuse to believe it.

(3) *The Bible exists to provide us with a reliable textbook of history, cosmology, geology, geography, biology, and other sciences.* Perhaps the most telling comment to be made upon

---

[3] Robert Richardson in *The Millennial Harbinger* (Bethany, Virginia, 1847), p. 700.

this assumption comes in the form of a news report in *Time* magazine:

## GALILEO: "A GREAT SPIRIT"

Three and a half centuries ago, the Vatican's Supreme Sacred Congregation of the Holy Office forbade the Italian Astronomer Galileo Galilei to "hold or defend" the Copernican theory, which Galileo's telescopes had verified, that the earth revolves around the sun rather than vice versa. Galileo stayed silent 16 years, then reasserted his view more strongly than ever in his *Dialogue on the Two Great World Systems.* In one of the world's most famous trials, the Roman Inquisition charged Galileo with heresy, threatened him with torture, and forced him to recant. This *Dialogue* was placed on the Index of Prohibited Books, and Galileo lived under house arrest and a revolving sun until his death in 1642.

The condemnation of Galileo has ever since been cited to demonstrate Roman Catholicism's opposition to science and free inquiry. Later, of course, it turned out to the satisfaction of everyone, including the Roman Catholic Church, that the earth does revolve around the sun. Galileo's works were removed from the Index in 1822, and a year ago French Jesuit François Russo suggested that the church might also formally repudiate the unjust censures directed at him.

Last week, at the National Catholic Eucharistic Congress in Pisa— where Galileo, according to legend, dropped a cannonball and a bullet from the leaning tower to prove that objects of different weight fall with the same velocity—Pope Paul VI formally praised Galileo, along with Dante and Michelangelo, as "great spirits" of "immortal memory."

It was a graceful tribute and a fitting one: the Pope whose Holy Office first condemned Galileo was Paul V.[4]

While there are few who would oppose the science of the Bible to that of modern physicists and biologists, there are still those

---

[4] June 18, 1965, p. 55. Courtesy *Time;* © Time Inc. 1965.

who have failed to make the same adjustment in their view of the Bible as a book of history. They continue to think of the Bible's historiography as intentionally contradicting that of modern history writers, and see the authority of the Bible as standing or falling on their defense. Not only is this defense unnecessary; it is woefully misguided.

(4) *The Bible exists to give magical protection to those who use it.* Thus, to have the Bible on a shelf or on a table in a home is supposed, by its simple presence, to bring God's blessing to that home—even if the sacred book is never read. A New Testament in the breast pocket of a soldier in battle has been credited with stopping a bullet from piercing his heart—not because it was a good paper shield but because it was a holy book. By simple extension, there is special merit in reading the Bible, whether the reader understands what he is reading or not. And similarly, there is favor with God from "believing in it," although the meaning of that phrase is highly ambiguous. There are those who extend this view of the Bible to the breaking point by using it as a lottery of answers to personal problems —letting it fall open by chance, dropping their finger or glance upon the open page, and reading it at that point as a modernized version of the Delphic Oracle.

The vein of superstition runs deep in the human mind; two thousand years of reasonable religion and the march of science have not been able to extirpate it. Superstition persists, and this view of the Bible is a part of it.

(5) *The Bible exists to give us correct creedal propositions.* This, of course, makes *faith* identical with *belief,* which it is not. The Bible itself repudiates such an identification: "You believe that God is one; you do well. [Obviously, this is meant to be read as sarcasm.] Even the demons believe—and shudder." (Jas. 2:19.) There are at least five counts against the down-

23

grading of faith into doctrine and reading the Bible primarily as a book of creeds or doctrines: (a) This view abstracts faith from the whole of life and makes it a matter of words and ideas. (b) It turns faith into a thing; it depersonalizes faith. (c) It makes faith a property to be cherished and defended with all the pride of ownership. (d) It divides believers of differing opinions from one another, sometimes even setting them against one another in holy wars. (e) By substituting a propositional dogma about God for personal communion with him, it even separates the believer from God himself. Such "faith" does not change men; it hardens them, makes them rigid and unteachable. It is not biblical.

In the five major assumptions about the Bible and the Word of God just reviewed, all identify the Bible as the Word of God, then make the Word identical with the words of the book. Their strength lies in the fact that all presuppose a divine revelation, and all make a transcendent claim upon human loyalty and allegiance in some sense. From that standpoint, they are psychologically sound; they assume that God is God and that man is not God.

Now turn in the opposite direction. The assumptions that follow presuppose no such revelation; these views are relatively humanistic, and they are just as inadequate as the five we have already sketched.

(6) *The Bible is a record of man's quest for God.* It is a valuable source book of the history of religion and the philosophy of religion. Perhaps more important, it shows us how our religious heritage in Christendom came into being, and it gives us a basis for our own religious thinking. Whatever nobility this view may have, it makes the edifice of religion nothing more than a human product, and it ignores the biblical view that God yearns for man, seeks him, and finds him; whereas

for the most part man not only does not seek God but actually flees from him.

(7) *The Bible exists as a cultural treasury of literary gems from an important part of antiquity.* It is a collection of folk literature from ancient Israel and the church in the early Roman period. As such it is valuable, as Homer's *Iliad* and *Odyssey* are valuable. As such, literary aesthetes drool over it and moan when translators dare to issue it in anything but the English of King James I. This view of the Bible regards it as a museum; and if there is a voice of God in it, it is a dying echo reverberating down long marble corridors.

### Toward an Adequate Answer

Before turning to a positive statement of the inherent purpose of the Bible from its own standpoint, we have had to dispose of several obstructing answers. Now the way is more nearly clear as we proceed to a more nearly adequate answer.

In simple, traditional terms, we may say that the Bible exists as a vehicle of salvation. As interpreted by nineteenth-century revivalism, that salvation was pictured largely in terms of life in heaven after physical death on earth. As interpreted by liberalism in the early decades of the present century, the saving work was construed in terms of "social salvation," "the Christianizing of the social order," or "the building of the kingdom of God on earth." Subsequent disillusionment with nineteenth-century revivalism and with the social gospel movement of the twentieth century has robbed many church members altogether of the message of salvation, even though that message remains the central thrust of the Bible. Obviously, the term "salvation" demands a reinterpretation at once closer to the Bible's own view and also more meaningful to the contemporary mind.

It is still true that the central work of the Bible is the salva-

25

tion of mankind. Nevertheless, the term "salvation" is semantically indigestible to modern man. The question, "Are you saved?" is liable to elicit the answering question, "Who is lost?" The lost-and-found analogy does not speak clearly to modern ears. It is not that modern man is not in need of rescue; it is rather that he does not habitually think of his predicament in those terms.

At this point it should be helpful to realize that the Bible speaks of its central work largely in the language of analogy. Fortunately it does not confine itself to one analogy, but uses several. A review of these shows some to be almost utterly foreign to modern ears, while others transmit their meaning with startling clarity. Consider a few of them.

*Ransom (redemption)*. Rooted in prehistory, the notion and practice of redemption as seen in the Torah was somehow tied to the idea that the firstborn of man and domestic animals were forfeit to death. Thus in Exod. 13:13; 34:20 and Num. 18:15-18, we encounter the law that the first female calf, the first lamb, and the first kid must be sacrificed to God on an altar, but that the first male calf and the first human child may be ransomed (bought back) by the payment of a redemption price. The reasoning behind this is inaccessible to the modern mind. Nevertheless, the fundamental analogy is clear: Man under sentence of death is ransomed, rescued, redeemed. At first this death is physical, but later it is understood to be spiritual, as in Rom. 8:2, "For the law of the Spirit of life in Christ Jesus has set me free from the law of sin and death."

When rooted in history, however, the notion of ransom becomes eminently clear. There are many Old Testament references to God's ransom of Israel from slavery in Egypt. Exod. 6:6 will serve as an example: "I will bring you out from under the burdens of the Egyptians, and I will deliver you from their

26

bondage, and I will redeem you with an outstretched arm." From this it is a natural step to the idea of ransom as deliverance from slavery in a spiritual sense:

> With him is plenteous redemption.
> And he will redeem Israel
> from all his iniquities— (Ps. 130:7-8) .

Deliverance from the bondage of sin in much the same sense is also seen in these terms as the central mission of Jesus: "For the Son of man also came not to be served but to serve, and to give his life as a ransom for many" (Mark 10:45) .

Paul's many references to bondage, slavery, and redemption therefore were probably rooted in the institution of human slavery as then practiced in the Roman Empire. Such references would have been meaningful to his contemporaries to a degree hardly possible for a modern audience one hundred years after the Emancipation Proclamation. For this reason, when the central purpose of the Bible and of the church is now stated in terms of this analogy, words like "redemption" and "ransom" are apt to convey little to modern minds. Such words frequently block communication; they rarely facilitate it unless interpreted.

*Blood atonement* (*propitiation, expiation, sacrifice*) . Here again we have human practices and ideas rooted in prehistory, the inner secrets of which remain profoundly inaccessible to the modern mind. Salvation in terms of analogies from the sacrificial system is prominent in the Bible for the simple reason that the sacrificial system was contemporary to the writing of both Testaments, in the Jewish world (prior to the destruction of the temple in A.D. 70) , and in the Gentile world. Not only is the whole of the book of Hebrews written from this analogy, but the figure frequently appears elsewhere. Consider a mere skimming of examples:

27

For there is no distinction; since all have sinned and fall short of the glory of God, they are justified by his grace as a gift, through the redemption which is in Christ Jesus, whom God put forward as an expiation by his blood, to be received by faith. (Rom. 3:22-25a.)

In him we have redemption through his blood, the forgiveness of our trespasses. (Eph. 1:7.)

And the blood of Jesus his Son cleanses us from all sin. (1 Jn. 1:7.)

> For thou wast slain and by thy blood
>     didst ransom men for God
> from every tribe and tongue and
>     people and nation. (Rev. 5:9.)

He entered once for all into the Holy Place, taking not the blood of goats and calves but his own blood, thus securing an eternal redemption. (Heb. 9:12.)

The same idea, attached to the Passover and to the Christian Eucharist, is expressed in I Cor. 5:7, "For Christ, our paschal lamb, has been sacrificed."

It seems probable that the modern mind will be forever at a loss to enter sympathetically into the reasoning behind the sacrificial system, and therefore unable fully to grasp the analogies built on it. The fundamental notion seems to be that of washing away the stain of sin—a soiling too deep to be got out with water. "Indeed, under the law almost everything is purified with blood, and without the shedding of blood there is no forgiveness of sins." (Heb. 9:22.)

In any case, let us not lose sight of the nature of the salvation presented through the analogy of the sacrificial system. It has to do with the removal of guilt, and it results in such lyrical passages as the following:

> Come now, let us reason together,
>     says the Lord:

28

> though your sins are like scarlet,
> they shall be as white as snow;
> though they are red like crimson,
> they shall become like wool  (Isa. 1:18).

*New creation (new birth, resurrection)*. A third strand of analogies for salvation to be found running through the Bible is that of creation and re-creation. The theme of all the passages using this figure in the Old Testament is sounded in the song of Second Isaiah:

> For behold, I create new heavens
> and a new earth;
> and the former things shall not be remembered
> or come into mind  (Isa. 65:17).

The entire ninety-seventh psalm is given to the singing of this theme. It is the theme of Isa. 9:2-7; 11:1-9 and of Rev. 21. But more importantly, it is the controlling image behind the lofty discourse of Jesus with Nicodemus on the housetop at night: "Truly, truly, I say to you, unless one is born anew, he cannot see the kingdom of God. . . . That which is born of the flesh is flesh, and that which is born of the Spirit is spirit. Do not marvel that I said to you, 'You must be born anew'" (John 3:3, 6-7). The analogy is also important to Paul. He uses it in II Cor. 5:17, "Therefore, if any one is in Christ, he is a new creation; the old has passed away, behold, the new has come." It is central to his discussion of baptism in Rom. 6:1-11. "We were buried therefore with him by baptism into death, so that as Christ was raised from the dead by the glory of the Father, we too might walk in newness of life." (Romans 6:4.) This figure is that of death and resurrection, which is new creation.

This analogy of renewal or new creation is less tied to

antiquity than the previous two. It will therefore prove more useful in communicating the message of salvation to our contemporaries.

*Healing.* Recovery from sickness commended itself to many prophets and biblical writers as an apt analogy for the work of salvation. Hence Hosea in the eighth century B.C. sang:

> Come, let us return to the Lord;
> for he has torn, that he may heal us;
> he has stricken, and he will bind us up (Hos. 6:1).

The figure is behind Jeremiah's famous lament:

> Is there no balm in Gilead?
> Is there no physician there?
> Why then has the health of the daughter of my people
> not been restored? (Jer. 8:22).

The same analogy appears elsewhere in Jeremiah, as for example in this petition:

> Heal me, O Lord, and I shall be healed;
> save me, and I shall be saved;
> for thou art my praise (Jer. 17:14).

The same idea lies behind passages like Ps. 41:4; Isa. 6:10; 27:18-19; Jer. 30:17; and many others. The crowning use of this analogy, however, waits for the New Testament and the compassionate figure of the Great Physician. "Those who are well have no need of a physician, but those who are sick; I have not come to call the righteous, but sinners to repentance." (Luke 5:31-32.)

This analogy is every bit as much at home in the twentieth century as it was in biblical times, perhaps more so. This is the day of psychosomatic medicine and of depth psychology. This is the Age of Anxiety, the place of Neurotic Culture. People suffer from neuroses, fixations, compulsions, and defense mechanisms. They flock for healing to the clinical psychologists, the marriage counselors, the psychiatrists and psychoanalysts in ever larger numbers. The analogy of salvation with healing is grooved for the main currents of our contemporary life. It is a biblical symbol—a powerful biblical symbol—which speaks directly and clearly to our age.

*Reconciliation (restoration of relationship).* The noun "reconciliation" and the verb "reconcile" appear in a relatively few passages and only in the New Testament.[5] Nevertheless, the analogy itself lies implicit behind many passages in both Testaments. When Hosea and Jeremiah speak of Israel's sin as infidelity and adultery, they are speaking of broken relationships between God and man, and calling for man to "be reconciled to God." When the prophets call for man to "turn" or "return," their call is informed by this thought.

In the contemporary setting this analogy opens the way for the theology of relationship which lies at the basis of the thought of such distinguished theologians as Martin Buber, Emil Brunner, Rudolf Bultmann, and Paul Tillich. When Tillich, for example, defines sin as estrangement—strained relationship—he is talking in these terms, and he is talking to ears that can understand. For this is the time of estranged and alienated people—at sixes and sevens within themselves, estranged from one another, and haunted by a sense of God's absence. In the notion of salvation as the restoration of broken or strained relationships we have another idea singularly timely in the present setting. It offers a ready channel for the transmission of biblical revelation.

[5] Eph. 2:16; Col. 1:20; Matt. 5:24; Rom. 5:10, 11; 11:15; II Cor. 5:18, 19, 20.

*Growing into maturity.* The word "mature," like "reconcile" and "reconciliation," appears only a few times in the New Testament, then mostly in the letters of Paul.[6] The same idea, though not the word, occurs in the famous hymn to love: "When I was a child, I spoke like a child, I thought like a child, I reasoned like a child; when I became a man, I gave up childish ways" (I Cor. 13:11).

In this day of intelligence quotients and personality quotients, of emotional immaturity and emotional maturation, we are ripe for the discussion of salvation as growth into maturity. Group evangelism and pastoral counseling relate naturally to it. By some curious psychology not fully explained, people who may be unwilling to think of themselves as in bondage, or as lost, let alone as sinners, are frequently willing to acknowledge that they are immature. In the analogy to human growth, especially in its emotional phase, we have a biblical symbol which may be readily conveyed to the modern mind.

There are still other biblical analogies for salvation—symbols such as *justification* (acquittal at court), *the kingdom of God, eternal life, abundant life, peace with God.* Limited space forbids their discussion here. Suffice it to say that the action of salvation is presented to us by the Bible in the language of analogy, but in itself salvation is no figure of speech. It is God's action meeting man's need. And it results in deepgoing changes in the life of man and society.

"Why does man need a revelation? Why does the Bible speak?" The answer, as we have seen, is not that we are in need of more information: Plato, Bacon, Aquinas, and Einstein have spoken; now let God speak and add to our knowledge. Most men are not scholars asking for knowledge in studies or laboratories. That is not where man is, nor who he is fundamentally.

[6] I Cor. 2:6; 14:20; Eph. 4:13; Phil. 3:15; Col. 1:28; 4:12.

We come much closer to his actual situation in a few phrases like these, all analogies: "strangers and pilgrims on earth," "no continuing city," "the night is dark and I am far from home."

For still another analogy and such light as it may cast, consider reflections of a man wandering down a forest path on a brilliant autumn afternoon: We are children of nature and we like to go back for a visit; but we are no longer at home there as are the groundhog, the redbird, and the squirrel. The innocence of nature, the sure, mindless instinct making thought unnecessary —we have been deprived of these in order that we may be compelled to look for a city that has foundations whose builder and maker is God. That is to say, we are being driven out into the world of spirit, where we must make choices and decisions and accept the responsibility for them. A chipmunk "knows" God and obeys him without thinking, for God is Lord over nature. But a man can choose to ignore God or deny him; for God has elected to be Lord not *over* man but Lord *of* man only by man's consent.

Such is the spiritual predicament of mankind—strangers on the earth, exiles from the realm of nature, but rebels and prodigals in the realm of the spirit. We are Abraham driven out of Ur; but we have gone only halfway to the promised land. We cannot go back; we lack the will to go forward. It is our destiny to be little lower than the angels; it is our fate that we often fall a great deal lower than the beasts. There is no human being who is not caught in this tragic tension—tragic because it involves the stark alternatives of man's destiny or his undoing. God in Christ has entered this tragic situation in order to speak to man in the midst of his pilgrimage; in order to be, if you please, the "kindly light amid the encircling gloom."

# 2

## The Bible and the Word of God

The Word of God is the Deed of God; the Deed of God is the Word of God. The gulf between words and deeds which characterizes men is overcome in God; what he says he does, and does immediately. This is the implication of the first account of creation: "And God said, . . . and it was so" (Gen. 1:9, 11).

Moreover, it may be taken as true that the Word of God is not audible language; it is not God talking in human words and with human voice. It is something more fundamental than that, something paradoxical, as expressed in the nineteenth psalm:

> Day to day pours forth speech,
>    and night to night declares knowledge.
>
> [*But*]
>
> There is no speech, nor are there words;
>    their voice is not heard;
>
> [*Nevertheless*]
>
> yet their voice goes out through all the earth,
>    and their words to the end of the world (Ps. 19:2-4).

The same paradox of speech and silence is found in the account of God's address to the prophet Elijah at the mouth of the cave

34

after the noisy earthquake, wind, and fire. The words translated "And after the fire a still small voice" (RSV) in Hebrew bear the connotation "the voice of a soft whisper" (Moffatt) or even "a voice of thin silence" (I Kings 9:12) .

Since "word" is so inadequate in conveying the meaning of the Word of God, we may wonder why the Bible uses it. Why not substitute Deed of God or His Mighty Acts, and by so doing erase the ambiguity of meaning in terms like the Word of the Lord and the voice of the Lord which are used so frequently in scripture?

The reason for preferring "word" to "deed," it would seem, lies in the deeper profundity and intimacy of the categories of language. A deed may be done alone, in isolation, but normally a man does not talk to himself; nor does he shout merely to hear his echo. Speech is communicative; it is the address of one person to another. This communicative, this loving aspect of God's deed is caught magnificently in the poem on creation by James Weldon Johnson. It is his presentation of a Negro sermon:

> And God stepped out on space,
> And he looked around and said:
> *I'm lonely—*
> *I'll make me a world. . . .*
> He looked on His world
> With all its living things,
> And God said: *I'm lonely still. . . .*
> Then God sat down—
> On the side of a hill where He could think;
> By a deep, wide river He sat down;
> With His head in His hands,
> God thought and thought,
> Till He thought: *I'll make me a man!* [1]

[1] "The Creation" from *God's Trombones* by James Weldon Johnson. Copyright 1927 by The Viking Press, Inc., 1955 by Grace Wail Johnson. Reprinted by permission of The Viking Press, Inc.

Thus in the mystery of language, with its call and response and its communion of heart with heart, we have a disclosure of the mystery of being. The first Word originates with God. Man's word is always an answering word. God speaks and man responds by coming into being. God speaks again and man responds in his moral nature by returning a "yes" or "no" to what God offers him and demands of him.

The Zürich theologian, Gerhard Ebeling, in an illuminating essay pursues this theme in the following words:

> Word is therefore rightly understood only when it is viewed as an event which—like love—involves at least two. The basic structure of word is therefore not statement—that is an abstract variety of the word event—but appraisal, certainly not in the colorless sense of information, but in the pregnant sense of participation and communication. . . .
>
> When word happens rightly, existence is illumined (and that naturally always means existence in association with others). . . . : the precise *purpose which the word is meant to serve is that man shows himself as man.* For that is his destiny. And for that reason word is absolutely necessary to man as man. For his destiny is to exist as response. He is asked what he has to say. He is not destined to have nothing to say and to have to remain dumb.[2]

God in his fundamental nature addresses man; man in his derived nature answers. God speaks; man responds. He is a responsible creature. And in this responsibility he finds his true character. It is for reasons like these that biblical talk about God uses the category of language in preference to the categories of deeds, ideas, or things.

[2] "Word of God and Hermeneutic," in *The New Hermeneutic,* ed. by James M. Robinson and John B. Cobb, Jr. (New York: Harper & Row, 1964), pp. 103, 104.

## The Word and the Words

At the same time we must be on guard against confusing the Word of God with words, even with the words of the Bible. From what we have already seen of the nonvocal but dynamic character of God's action through his Word, we have to say that it is a Word before all words and all worlds. It is the Word which adumbrates beneath, around, through, and above all words. It is the Word that outlasts all words and persists eternally—the Alpha and the Omega, world without end. For the Word of God is the self-communication of the living God eternally in interaction with his creation. It is God himself— not the Bible—who creates, provides, makes moral claims, judges, instructs, forgives, heals, and commissions. And the Word of God is his creating, sustaining, claiming, judging, saving, and commissioning activity; it is nothing less than this. As such the Word is addressed; and it calls for an answer. Man is on the other end of it—called into being by it, called to account by it, rescued from falsehood by it, and by it sent forth to serve.

This living and active Word cannot suffer reduction to cold print. It is not identical with the sum total of the words of the Bible, though it infuses these words. It is not a special residue of divine words which remain after all the human words of the Bible have been sifted out. All the words of the Bible are the words of men, even though they bear witness to the Word of God.

Nor does the Bible contain the Word of God as a vessel holds a liquid, the assumption being that outside the Bible there is no Word of God. A classic statement for the kind of theological positivism which limits the Word of God to the Bible is that of the nineteenth-century reformer Alexander Campbell, in his *Christian System*. In what he says he echoes the philosopher John Locke, and in some ways prefigures Karl Barth:

The Bible is to the intellectual and moral world of man what the sun is to the planets in our system—the fountain and source of light and life, spiritual and eternal. There is not a spiritual idea in the whole human race that is not drawn from the Bible. As soon will the philosopher find an independent sunbeam in nature, as the theologian a spiritual conception in man, independent of THE ONE BEST BOOK.[3]

A statement as extravagant as this comes dangerously close to bibliolatry. It almost dethrones God and puts a book in his place. What is more, it flies directly into the face of God's self-revelation to nonbiblical people as mentioned by Paul:

For what can be known about God is plain to them, because God has shown it to them. Ever since the creation of the world his invisible nature; namely, his eternal power and deity, has been clearly perceived in the things that have been made. So they are without excuse (Rom. 1:19, 20; see also 2:12-16).

Besides which, the Word of God is presented in the Bible itself as in several phases prebiblical: "By the word of the Lord the heavens were made" (Ps. 33:6) —long before writing had been invented! "Now the word of the Lord came to me," said Jeremiah (Jer. 1:4), years before he dictated his book to Baruch the scribe, (Jer. 36). "And the Word became flesh and dwelt among us" (John 1:14), a generation before any part of the New Testament came to be written, and more than three centuries before the New Testament assumed its present form as a canon.

What, then, is the relation between the Word of God and the words of the Bible?

[3] Alexander Campbell, *The Christian System in Reference to the Union of Christians and a Restoration of Primitive Christianity as Plead in the Current Reformation.* (St. Louis: Bethany Press, 1922), p. 15.

## Calvin, Luther, and Tillich

A somewhat literalistic approach to this question is that of John Calvin, whose logical mind detected three stages of the Word. To begin with, Jesus Christ is the Word of God. This is the simple assertion of the prologue to the Fourth Gospel. Next, the Bible is the Word of God in a secondary or derivative sense because it is about Christ. The Old Testament is as christo-centric as the New, according to Calvin's thought, because it leans forward in anticipation of Christ's coming. At still a second removal, the third stage, preaching is the Word of God —derivatively—because it is from the Bible. The Bible is the source, the standard for the criticism of preaching. Thus the spoken word of the pulpit is the servant of the written word in the Bible, which in turn is the servant of the true, living, orig-inal, and everlasting Word of God in Christ. Preaching becomes the living word by mediating Christ through the Bible. To do this the Word needs the Holy Spirit "to bore the ears" of the listener so that he may receive the Word in its own terms as living and active, mighty to save.[4]

Martin Luther was less literalistic. For him the Word of God was the Deed of God. All the concrete, created things of the world are words of God. All the events of history are words of God. But the central events of history are two in number, and they form the core of the two Testaments—the event of the Exodus for the Old Testament, the event of Christ for the New.

Luther discerned the Word of God in three stages: (1) *The Creative Word.* By his Word God created the world. Before creation, said Luther, God was like a man who walks along a street talking to himself. Then, suddenly, he shouted; everyone knew then what he had been saying all along.

---

[4] Leroy Nixon, *John Calvin, Expository Preacher* (Grand Rapids: William B. Eerdmans Publishing Co., 1950), pp. 49-56.

(2) *The Redemptive Word*. This is Christ, the second person of the Trinity. This is the Word of John's prologue. The need for such a Word lies in man's sinfulness; man in his bound condition is in need of a liberator. God, on his part, has built redemption into the very structure of the universe, so that even the trees and the birds speak of the forgiveness of God. But, centrally, he has spoken his redemptive Word in Christ. The Bible is the Word of Christ because it is the book of Christ. Christ is the center of the Old Testament, not merely because the Old Testament predicts his coming, but because in his divine preexistence Christ the Savior worked covertly in the deliverance of the Israelites from bondage and did all the other redeeming acts of the Old Covenant. And, obviously, Christ is the center of the New Testament not covertly, but explicitly and openly.

(3) *The Word of God spoken by Christ is identical with the Word of God now spoken by the church through preaching*. Luther's strong bent toward action shows in his insistence that the Word of God had to come through the actual voice of the preacher in communicating with a congregation; for, as he said, the church is not a *Federhaus* (pen-house) but a *Mundhaus* (mouth-house). The Word of Christ is made contemporary through such preaching by the third person of the Trinity, the Holy Spirit.[5]

Contemporary theologian Paul Tillich discerns six meanings in the term "Word of God." (1) It is the principle of divine self-manifestation of God himself in his own character. It is God's nature to reveal himself, for he is "not only an abyss in

---

[5] Jaroslav Pelikan, ed. *Luther, the Expositor: Introduction to the Exegetical Writings* (St. Louis: Concordia Publishing House, 1959), pp. 48-70.

which every form disappears," but is also "the source from which every form emerges."

(2) It is the medium of creation by which God brings "concrete, individualized, self-related" spiritual beings into existence (as contrasted with mechanical things emanating from an impersonal fullness).

(3) It is "the manifestation of divine life in the history of revelation. It is the word received by all those who are in a revelatory correlation." This, presumably, is the word spoken by the prophets in times past, the word that came to Israel under the Old Covenant.

(4) It is the final revelation in Jesus as the Christ. "The Word is not the sum of the words spoken by Jesus. It is the being of the Christ, of which his words and his deeds are an expression."

(5) Though not identical with the Bible, the Word is related to the Bible in two senses: (a) The Bible is "the document of the final revelation," and (b) "it participates in the final revelation of which it is the document."

(6) It is the proclamation of the church, justly called the Word of God, if and when at least four factors come together in "a constellation": (a) the meaning in the words spoken; (b) the power with which these words are spoken; (c) the understanding and existential receptivity of the hearer (he must take them into his life, not merely into his mind); (d) the correlation or interaction of preacher and listener in true communion with each other.[6]

In the foregoing review of three distinguished Protestant thinkers of past and present, we come upon certain basic agreements. Laying aside for the moment a consideration of the Creative Word, we see that the major emphasis of the

[6] Paul Tillich, *Systematic Theology* (Chicago: The University of Chicago Press, 1951), I, 157-59.

Bible is upon the Redemptive Word. This is fully manifest in the person and work of Christ. But it is present wherever God's saving activity goes forward.

The Bible is important because through it we are able to meet the living Christ. In our own way we may say that the Bible is the record, the witness, of men in times past to God's saving activity. As a record, however, the Bible is not a mere court record—it is a literary record which participates in the power of the events that it records. It has the capacity to elicit in the reader and the hearer the kind of response that Christ first drew forth from those who knew him in the flesh. Far from being a dead letter—that is, when read in faith by the light of God's present Spirit—the Bible is living and life-giving. It surges with contemporaneity. It makes Christ contemporary. It confronts us with the living God.

### God in History

Underlying this view of the redemptive activity of God there is one tremendous assumption: The fundamental sphere of God's redemptive self-disclosure is history—a particular history of a particular people; the particular history of a particular human being. This view of the matter stands over against every form of gnosticism and mysticism. Though we may not deny that man can come to know something about God through human reasoning or that he may come into communion with him in ecstatic vision, the Bible is predicated upon the assumption that the central normative manifestation of God to man is conveyed in the history of the Jews, and more especially in the history of one Jew, the crown and summation of the whole Israelite story. This is a bold assertion, but it is not more illogical than its contrary. There is no reason why God should not disclose himself in events rather than in ideas, or in persons rather than in ecstatic visions.

Taking the Word of God in its redemptive manifestation in history, we can discern in the Bible three phases of the saving Word of God as it comes to us.

1. In its first phase the Word of God is an act in history, a unique and unrepeatable complex of events. For the Old Testament this is the deliverance of Israel from Egyptian bondage, the making of the covenant, and the giving of the law. For the New Testament this Deed was the life, teachings, death, and resurrection of Jesus Christ, and the coming of the Holy Spirit to the church.

2. In its second phase the Word of God is the life of God in the midst of his people. It is the saving life of the covenant community. This community creates the Scriptures as one expression of its life with God. And since the Scriptures rose as the record of that life, and welled up from the source of inspiration, it has always the capacity of quickening the life of the Spirit for those who come to it in faith. Here we need to stress the fact that the covenant community to which the Bible is related is not merely the church of the ancient past; it is the living community, a mighty cable of life, stretching out of the long past, gathering us into its vital strands in this present hour, and stretching on into God's future. The Bible rose in the church; when it is read in faith it claims us for the church, which is to say that it quickens us to the rebirth by which we may enter the community of God's people or it calls us back through repentance to a renewal of the bonds that we have broken. To open the Bible as a book of faith is to open and pass through the door into the covenant community.

3. The third phase of the life of God's Word as it comes to us we have already discussed as an integral part of the second phase. But, while it may not be separated in experience, we can discuss it separately. Neither the Deed of God nor his life in the covenant community can be the Word of God for us until it

43

comes home to us and takes us captive, heart and soul. To put it as Acts does of Pentecost, we must be "pricked in our hearts" by it. The Word must become a personal word calling us by name. God does not tyrannize the human heart; he does not break and enter. He does not coerce. He persuades, which means that he always asks for human consent. Without the human response, the Word of God comes to naught. This means that the Bible needs more than inspired writers. It needs inspired *readers*. In fact, without human response we cannot even hear the word as the Word. A man who receives the Word is not like a person who has picked up a bundle; he has not added *something* he did not have before. Rather he has entered into a new relationship with God, and hence with his fellows and with himself. Henceforth he is not his own, but God's. And he has not something but someone; or, to put it more accurately, Someone has him, and he is born anew.[7]

This third phase, highly individual and immediate, is, in the fine wording of Emil Brunner, "The Divine-Human Encounter." It is meeting. It is the fundamental dialogue in which God speaks and man answers. History is the sphere of God's revelation even here, for God comes to a man in the events of his personal history. When God speaks to us in this meeting or dialogue he speaks to us *live,* not merely in a tape recording or a paper recording, he himself being elsewhere and otherwise occupied at the moment. For that reason it may be helpful to think of the sacred writings—the record—in the Bible as a catalytic agent stimulating man in such a way that the live interaction between him and God really takes place. In the Word of God it is not a report but God himself who comes to us.

And when God comes to us he comes not as an equal, on a

[7] The forgoing three paragraphs are repeated from my book *Preaching on the Books of the Old Testament* (New York: Harper & Row, 1961), pp. 7-8.

horizontal plane. When he comes he comes as Lord. He himself comes. He comes with a claim upon us, demanding to be our Lord. The realization of this reaches us, registers, and leaves its mark first in the realm of moral law, through our breach of it. We stand before God as convicted lawbreakers. Our efforts to hide, to flee, to justify ourselves, to restore our primitive innocence take many forms, all of which finally fail. So long as God comes to us only in the guise of creator, lawgiver and judge, we are under condemnation and there is no hope for us. But when God meets us as Redeemer, which he does through the salvation-history of Israel and of Jesus Christ, and through the truth as spoken in the love of a concerned community, we may dare to believe that God is for us and not against us. We can risk having the whole ground of our existence torn from beneath us as we confess our sins, trust in his love, and accept his healing. Then it is, and not until then, that it becomes possible for us to know God as Father and as spiritual Presence.

# 3

## Some Presuppositions in
## Biblical Interpretation

All human beings hold presuppositions on a number of subjects
—for example, on the relation of the earth to the solar system;
on monarchy, dictatorship, and democracy; on marriage; on
making money. Ordinarily presuppositions of any sort have
a dual character. They are assumed, taken for granted, hence
precede conscious judgments, and as such, usually lie beneath
the conscious processes of reason in those who hold them. This
means that they also preclude argument; that we tend to be
dogmatic about them; that they generate enormous emotional
power. In fact, they control our frontage upon life.

It is therefore not surprising that no one reads the Bible or
approaches it in any manner without his own presuppositions,
whether he is aware of them or not. These constitute the "mind
set," or the standpoint from which one's perspective upon scripture is determined. By their inherent nature they limit or
liberate understanding. It is, in consequence, urgently important
to probe for them, to discover them, and to bring them up into
the light of awareness. "The uncriticized life is not worthy to be
lived by man." This dictum of Socrates is as applicable to
thought about the Bible as it is to anything else. An uncriticized
frontage upon the Bible is unworthy of the serious student of

46

the Bible. Conscientious study of the Bible includes the obligation of discovering one's own presuppositions about the Bible, and it should go on to the criticism, cleansing, and clarification of those presuppositions.

One way of finding one's own presuppositions is by probing for and discussing the assumptions of others. We discover our own fundamental opinions by reacting—in agreement or disagreement—to the presuppositions of others. It is for this reason, and in the spirit of dialogue, that I offer the following assumptions of my own, so far as I have been able to articulate them:

(1) To begin with, the Bible is a record of a series of past meetings between God and men within the history of a particular people, the Israelites. The events of this past history climaxed in the life history of a single Israelite, Jesus of Nazareth. What we see when we turn to the Bible is first of all a story of what happened long ago, as remotely as three or four thousand years ago, and as recently as nineteen hundred years ago. Seen in this first light, as a record from antiquity, everything in the Bible happened "a long time ago; far, far away."

(2) These events in the biblical record are to be seen, however, as central to all history for all peoples. The Bible assumes that the history of the Israelites and of the New Israel, the church, is not simply one more history to be laid down beside the history of other peoples, but that it is central, pivotal to all other histories. Thus history is rescued from being

> a tale
> Told by an idiot, full of sound and fury,
> Signifying nothing.

Israel and the church, to be sure, are not the rulers of other peoples, but servants, destined to be suffering servants, for the

47

healing of the nations. The center of this central history is God giving himself for man on the Cross. The goal of history is the future coming of this Crucified One in power.

(3) Although the canon of scripture was closed about nineteen hundred years ago for the Old Testament and about sixteen hundred years ago for the New Testament, the biblical story is not finished. It is a continuing story embracing an apostolic community—people who are sent to the world in the great commission. As such we are within the biblical drama. We are commissioned to serve between the ascension and the return of Christ (however that return is interpreted).

(4) The power by which we live, if we are truly within the church, is the power of the Holy Spirit, who first came to the church at Pentecost and whose steadfast love never lets us go. This Holy Spirit is God himself, the spiritual Presence, grasping us, inspiring us, transforming us.[1] This Holy Spirit has the power of making Christ contemporary, of effecting a personal meeting in which God claims us for himself. The Holy Spirit may do this through scripture, not in any magical way but catalytically, using the living history of the past to stimulate a living response to God in the present moment.

(5) The purpose of biblical interpretation is to enable the Bible to perform this catalytic function for the reader or hearer, so that God himself will come to us in living terms, speaking to each of us in his own individual situation. This meeting of God and person may never be wholly predicted in advance. It may not be controlled by the biblical interpreter and is not in man's categories but in God's. In spite of fine phrases to the contrary, no man speaks for God to another man. God speaks for himself. The words of men, even those in scripture and certainly those of the preacher, are at best instrumental. They

[1] Paul Tillich, *The Eternal Now* (New York: Charles Scribner's Sons, 1963), p. 84.

can never be coercive to man or to God, though God may use them as the channel of his self-revealing and healing act in the life of a man.

(6) The words of the Bible are the words of men. These words bear witness to the Word of God, which is his Deed, never reducible to any verbal formula, but always calling for a response on the part of those whom God claims through his Deed. The words of the Bible are not, singly or in sum, identical with the Word of God, though the Word of God uses the words in doing his work in, with, and for man.

(7) Because the Bible consists of the words of the men who wrote it and is the record of the imperfect response of man to God's summons, it has peaks and valleys. Though it everywhere points to its own highest fulfillment in Christ, it is not everywhere Christian in its morality or theological insight. When Samuel chopped King Agag of the Amalekites into bits as a human sacrifice to God, he was doing something savage and primitive, hardly acceptable to a conscience educated by Christ and the apostles. Nahum's hate-filled denunciation of Nineveh and Obadiah's diatribe against Edom have within them no flicker of love for enemies, such as Christ enjoined in Matt. 5. The Bible in its parts must be corrected in the light of the whole. This means that particular verses and passages must be read contextually, the ultimate context being nothing less comprehensive than the mind of Christ.

(8) Even the truth of the Bible has to be received by the hearer or reader in order to become his truth. This means that there will be variety, even conflict, in the conceptualizations of the Word as received by the same person at different times and by different persons at the same time. The Word is saved from utter subjectivism, however, by the objectivity of God's Mighty Acts, which are events in history, and also by the nature of man, who is made in God's image and who therefore has an

objective requirement in his inner life. That objective norm is full maturity, measured by Christ. Moreover, the response of man to God's Word is not static, but living and dynamic. It involves *growth* toward Christlikeness and is never satisfied with fixed opinions or rigid positions.

(9) Although the Bible is a call to the individual person, it calls him into community. It is personal, but not private in the isolated, unilateral sense. On the contrary, the biblical Word binds people to each other—love of God implies love of neighbor, and, more than that, service of God operates within a covenantal community. After all, the Bible is the book of the two covenants; it is the book of the church. The living Bible, wherever it is taken seriously, calls the church into being, or where the church already exists, purges and renews it. The Bible is therefore best read and understood in the light of the inter-personal life of those who have made their covenant with God and neighbor. This is an added safeguard against subjective relativity; when men stand before God they stand together. They come together in study, in worship, in fellowship, and in service. By their life together they correct each other. The Word of the Bible is also, and at the same time, the Word to the church.

(10) The fundamental appeal of the Bible is not to fact but to faith and to the faith-surrender. The Bible is read at its depth only in faith. It is understood only in repentance. It is fully received only in self-forgetful service born of love toward God and man. This means, in the words of Rudolf Bultmann, that "the hearing of the word of the Bible can take place only in personal decision," and that "I can understand love only by loving." [2]

(11) To the extent that a passage of scripture becomes a

[2] *Jesus Christ and Mythology* (New York: Charles Scribner's Sons, 1958), pp. 57-58.

channel for the Word of God, it probes the reader or hearer. This is a reversal of the relationship of reader to book in ordinary realms of knowledge. Ordinarily the reader probes the passage, tries to understand it, judges it to be true or false, dissects it, analyzes it, accepts or rejects it. In the reading of the Bible all this is reversed. The passage probes the man, judges him to be true or false, calls him to repentance and decision. With ordinary books the reader interprets the text; with the Bible the text interprets the man.

That is to say, the Word of God addresses the conscience. No one has said this more penetratingly than Gerhard Ebeling in his essay on "Worldly Talk of God":

The only responsible talk of God is that which aims at the place where God and the world meet as it were in a mathematical point. That place is the conscience. Because responsible talk of God aims at the conscience, the world necessarily also becomes a question when talk of God stands in question. For conscience sake we cannot speak of God without speaking of the world. For as conscience man stands between God and the world. . . .

It is true that our talk of God aims solely at the inmost being, the conscience. But precisely what happens in the inmost part has the outmost effects. The nature of man's inmost being, his conscience, is grasped only when it is clearly realized that here it is not a case of man in the abstract, separated from the world, and of his then necessarily likewise abstract relation to God; rather, the conscience is, as we said already, the place where God and the world meet. If our talk of God is aimed at faith, then faith, because it has to do with God, has to do with the world. And *the conscience is only really affected when our talk of God concretely pins man down,* but also frees him, at the point where he thinks himself free but is actually bound, or also where he considers himself bound but is actually free. Speaking of God does not suffer the concrete point at which we exist in the world to be forgotten; but when it is done

51

in truth, then its authority lies in the fact that *it lays a finger on that concrete point and therefore calls things by their true names, summons them forth from concealment, brings them out of darkness into light, and thereby sets them in motion and puts them to work.* Then, for example, "sin" is no longer a pious term—sin leaps at us. And then "forgivenness" is no longer an edifying phrase, but the coming of that freedom which changes the face of the world.[3]

(12) There are many legitimate ways of reading the Bible which neither seek nor find it a channel for the Word of God. It may be read for the light it throws upon the history of vanished empires, for its correlations with the sciences of anthropology and archaeology. It may be approached as a kind of museum of social institutions and customs. It may be seen as a library of literary types and read strictly as literature. It may be studied for the purity of its text in the light of its transmission through manuscripts and versions from the times of antiquity until the present. Its books may be submitted to the scrutiny of the most exacting historical criticism as to authorship, time, place, circumstances and purpose of writing. And there are still other possible, pre-*logos* approaches to the Bible.

All these approaches are permissible, even desirable, but they are preliminary to and fall short of being a study of the Bible as the record of God's Word and the channel of his direct address to the reader. The books of the Bible were not written for these preliminary purposes, but rather for the ultimate purpose of confronting man, in conscience, with the living God. The interpretation of scripture which is to be taken

---

[3] *Word and Faith,* tr. by James W. Leitch (Philadelphia: Fortress Press, 1963), pp. 356, 360. Italics mine.

seriously in the life of the church addresses itself to nothing less than this ultimate purpose. At the same time, it will learn all it can from the preliminary studies, so as not to fly away into undisciplined hunches and fancies.

(13) There are many varieties of literature in the Bible. To interpret any of them it is necessary to know the basic norms for that type of literature. One check list from a college text on the literary study of the Bible contains no less than sixteen literary forms, such as: folk songs, myths, legends, short stories, parables, fables, allegories, biographies, history, laws, poetry (including patriotic songs, elegies, and love lyrics), drama, proverbs, speeches, prayers, letters, and essays. Obviously, a poem is not to be read by the same canons of interpretation as a law; a parable is not an allegory; and a prayer and a love song are not to be confused with each other. In some quarters there is a determined effort to force all biblical literature into the single mold of factual history. This coercive approach does great violence to biblical forms, and hence to the biblical meanings to be read from them. Before a passage of scripture can be understood, the reader must know what type of literature he is dealing with and he must have some skill in applying the canons of that type.

(14) To speak to any hearer or reader the Bible must be translated into his tongue and thought forms. Until this is done it is Hebrew and Greek to him, in a double sense. Both its words and its meanings remain foreign to him.

The work of verbal translation has been done by experts. It is a treasure ready to hand in the many excellent modern-speech versions such as those of Goodspeed, Moffatt, the RSV, the NEB, and the renderings of J. B. Phillips. Even so, there are elusive qualities of language which can never be captured in translation. For the exegete who will take the trouble to "dig it out" in the original tongues of Hebrew and Greek there are unsuspected riches in most biblical passages not made fully available in any translation.

The work of cultural translation from the thought forms of antiquity to the thought forms of the twentieth-century West is much more difficult. The previous chapter, in discussing the biblical analogies for salvation, dealt with certain aspects of this task. The cosmology, the demonology, the astrology, and the political science of the biblical writers are radically different from the world view of the twentieth century. It is the task of theology to rescue the abiding essence of scripture from the changing and outmoded envelope in which it is conveyed. This task of cultural translation was actually begun before the New Testament canon was closed, as witness the Johannine writings and the Epistle to the Hebrews, which are translations of the gospel from the thought forms of the Jews into those of the Greeks. The phrase "kingdom of God," "kingdom of heaven," or its synonym "kingdom," to give only one example, is used more than one hundred times in the Synoptic Gospels, but it almost disappears in the Gospel of John, where it is displaced by "eternal life," "life abundant," and "life."

This process of cultural translation, like that of verbal translation, is never finished. It has to be done anew in each situation. Without it the Word of God is only an echo from a no longer living past.

There is still another aspect of this matter of cultural translation. To fail to bring it off is to shift the offense of scripture from its rightful place—in the stubborn self-idolatry of the hearer—to matters of secondary importance. That is, a hearer may be offended by the seeming conflict of science and religion rather than by the unwelcome truth that he is a sinner who needs to repent.

(15) As superb literature the Bible is a mirror. Most of the men and women whom we see there are reflections. We can see ourselves mirrored there. The hearer of the sermon or reader of the Bible does not need to be smuggled into the passage. He is already there in the passage. This is possible because of the dynamics of psychological identification, such as that experienced by a spectator at a play with an actor on the stage, or that of a reader of a novel with its hero.

(16) Although the Word of God is meant to heal and to build, it wounds before it heals, it roots up before it plants, it wrecks before it builds. Without the judgment of God personally received there can be no action of the saving grace of God. For this reason the figurative description of the Word of God as the Sword of the Spirit is especially appropriate. We might translate that into a surgeon's scalpel. The thing that ails us will not be cured by moral poultices. We need surgery. But after surgery there can be healing and restoration to health.

(17) The Bible is not the sole channel of God's redemptive work among men, for it is God himself who redeems. But God's work with men is not fully illumined apart from the Bible. This is because the Bible is preeminently the book of Christ, and in Christ, God's purpose and action are fully stated for all time. *Limiting God*

To insist, however, that no Christian sermon can be preached without using a particular passage of scripture as a text is mistaken and misleading. It is to identify the living Word of God too closely with the words of the Bible and to limit God too narrowly. Nevertheless, the preacher who can be trusted with a topical sermon is the man who is so thoroughly immersed in a knowledge of the Bible that he may prefer to preach from a particular passage. Given a living faith and not a stultifying, literalistic legalism, a text is liberating, not limiting. It saves a preacher from abstractions and generalities; it gives him the power of the concrete and the specific, without which the spirit, like Noah's dove from the ark, flies to and fro and finds no place to alight.

(18) The Word of God is not a general revelation, like a radio broadcast. It is a personal Word coming afresh to each man in a face-to-face meeting. It is personally addressed to him, and to him alone. God calls him by name, not by number. The Word of God comes to a man not once in a lifetime but frequently, meeting him in new and unrepeatable situations as his life unfolds in daily actions and events. The Word through preaching can illumine these events, open them, make them accessible to the Spirit so that the action of the sermon, like the action of the Bible upon which it is based, is not limited to the time of reading and of preaching, but follows a man home and to work, where God waits to speak anew.

In all of this the Word of God is not to be coerced. God is not to be ordered about by us. One suspects that one motive for a return to the Bible in our time may be the very human but sinful desire to get God under our control—to cram his living Word into our tiny system of words—so as to achieve a kind of emotional security that the immature are always seeking. However great the temptation, we must never place ourselves in the position of being "Lord of the Scriptures," forcing them to speak a certain meaning to all men at the same time, or to the same man at different times. "True authority," one has said, "is an act of grace. And the grace of God is free. . . . No man has the power to summon the presence of the Word of God. Here the preacher is distinguished from the sorcerer who thinks that he can compel God by chanting formulas." [4]

[4] Walter Lüthi and Eduard Thurneysen, *Preaching: Confession: The Lord's Supper,* tr. by Francis J. Brooke, III (Richmond: John Knox Press, 1960), pp. 12-13.

Anyway, I suspect that biblical revelation frequently brings us no answer to our questions but only a deeper, more persistent question—like the fire in the bones of Jeremiah. And fundamentally it brings us neither answer nor question, but instead conducts us into a Presence who speaks to and for us with sighs too deep for words.

# 4

## The Minister as a Biblical Student

Every parish minister is the biblical scholar of his congregation, as he is the theologian, the preacher, and the pastor of that congregation. This is in direct contradiction to the erstwhile specialization that separated scholarship from preaching a few years ago.

Both academicians and pastors contributed to that unfortunate separation. Theologians wrote books for each other, or appeared to do so. Biblical scholars delved into studies so technical and so remote from parish interests that they appeared to have no concern for the ongoing life of a local church. They further seemed to assume that their life of scholarship stood apart from the involvements of churchmanship—they need not themselves be preachers or even participating members of local congregations. Theirs could be—though it seldom was—a life of the pure intellect isolated in academic solitude.

Preachers, on their side, supposed the atmosphere of such lofty study to be too rarefied for them. Their many parish tasks kept them busy. They had little time for what the cloistered scholars had to say; besides, they could not always understand these intellectuals when they did take time to read or listen. Thus exegesis and homiletics drifted apart—exegesis eventuat-

ing in an impersonal rendition of the text abstracted from the
faith of the church, and homiletics flying off into "preach-
ments" seldom disciplined by sound theological thinking and
hard biblical study.

This great gulf between scholarship and preaching must
be bridged. Ever since Karl Barth wrote and published his
epochal commentary on Romans at the end of World War I,
scholarship has been working at this bridging operation. Barth
was driven both to theology and to exegesis, in fact, by the
torment of his pulpit task. It was as a parish minister that he
undertook this study which has done so much, in turn, to set
the mood of scholarship for a whole generation. The scholarly
detachment of the old liberalism is gone; it is now almost universally understood by the scholars that knowledge and faith
cannot be separated, that understanding requires commitment,
that there is no insight into the literature of the church and
the thought of the church without complete immersion into the
life of the church. Besides, ever since C. H. Dodd's little book
on *The Apostolic Preaching and Its Developments* was published in 1936, biblical literature itself has been seen as proclamation—kerygmatic preaching.

It is now the preacher's turn to work at bridge building.
In fact, many local pastors are already hard at work on this
bridging operation. Although the minister may not be the
front line scholar of the church, he is the biblical scholar,
the theologian, as well as the educator, the pastor, the ad-
ministrator, the priest, and the preacher of his congregation.
If he abdicates his scholarly function, his congregation will have
no mentor in these affairs.

At the very least, a local minister is obliged to be the
middleman between the scholarly specialist and the churchman
in the pew. He is the theological and exegetical money changer,
as it were; his task is to take the thousand-dollar bills of special-

59

ized theology and change them into nickels, dimes, quarters, dollars, and ten-dollar bills, so that the people can do business with these ideas in the workaday world. In the middleman's role he now has the help of a growing body of literature in such volumes as Christian World Books, the Layman's Theological Library, Reflection Books, the Christian Faith Series, and many others ostensibly addressed to laymen. New commentaries which unite exegesis and exposition are also coming from the press. It is now possible, as it has not been for two generations, to heal the breach between the church's head and its heart. Whether this happens or not will depend primarily on local ministers.

If the rift between scholarship and preaching is to be healed, preachers will have to learn to curb their penchant for quick "sermonizing" and submit to the disciplines of biblical study. The secret is to resist the urge to organize a passage quickly. First let the minister as preacher become wholly absorbed in the minister as student. Let him then turn to the homiletical implications of the text, but not until then. His preaching will be the stronger for this preliminary work, having the sound undergirding of hermeneutics and exegesis. His work in the pulpit will take on depth. The people will look up to him and be fed.

Whether or not a given preacher takes this bridge-building task seriously will depend, at the bottom, upon a new way of working which can be separated into steps developed into a weekly pattern. Obviously there is no one way of doing this— one man's method may be another man's chaos, but method there must be. The task must be divided into its parts, and these parts must be tackled one after the other.

It now falls to me, as author, to suggest a pattern for such study. I do so with some diffidence, knowing that it is only one pattern among many possible patterns. And yet, because several

60

generations of seminary students have tested our pattern and found it helpful, I am made bold enough to set it forth with some confidence. It is not necessary to tell the reader that he may modify it, adapt it, or even discard it and devise his own. Nevertheless, it is offered for such concrete stimulus and help as it may be able to deliver.

## *1.* Choose the Text

The first task is to select the passage which is to be the text of the sermon. Homiletical custom, hallowed by long usage, seems to decree that the text shall be short—barely a verse or two—a small enough packet to be carried easily in the memory. In keeping with this notion, homiletical theory has been accustomed to distinguish between *textual* and *expository* preaching. The basis for the distinction has been simply that of length; "textual" preaching was based upon a short text, "expository" preaching upon a long one. Textual preaching was accepted as the rule; expository preaching became the exception—the rare exception—highly desirable but seldom undertaken and even less frequently achieved.

In recent years it has become my growing conviction that this traditional distinction between textual and expository preaching is superficial and that it ought to be discarded. Scripture is not properly measured by the inch or the mile. There are single verses—as in the sayings of Jesus—worth whole books such as Obadiah; but there are other single verses which in themselves say nothing. Obviously, the criterion of choice should not be length but significance. All that is necessary is that the text—long or short—shall be a unit, and that it shall be somewhere near the center and not on the margins of the biblical world.

There are many possible units of scripture which serve as good texts for sermons. There are episodes, discourses, parables,

61

allegories, miracle stories, psalms, folk songs, biographical tales (some exceedingly brief and others running through many chapters and even beyond one biblical book), letters, speeches, prayers, laws. And there are the biblical books themselves, the most natural units of scripture imaginable—and the most neglected in the shaping of sermons.[1]

It would also seem axiomatic that the choosing of a text should not be "catch as catch can" from Sunday to Sunday, but that it should be against the background of conscious design gathering at least a year into its plan. The aim of such design should be comprehensiveness and balance. It should draw upon the Old Testament as well as the New, upon the Prophets as well as the Writings and the Laws; upon the Gospel as well as the Epistles. It should cover the full spectrum of biblical doctrines from creation to eschatology. It should be kerygmatic as well as ethical.

There are several plans of biblical reading and study which are ready at hand. There are the periscopes of the Christian Year, the liturgical units to be found in Lutheran and Episcopal prayer books and in other books of common worship devised by several of the less liturgical churches. Some of these are organized to cover nearly the whole of the Bible within five years. The International Bible Lessons for Christian Teaching— the "Uniform Lessons"—not only divide scripture into weekly units but also run in six-year cycles inclusive of nearly the whole of the Bible. Some preachers use them at times other than on assigned Sundays with the church school to supply the framework of their preaching programs. Closely allied to it are the daily Bible readings devised by the American Bible Society and the Bible Reading Plan for Christian Men and Women pre-

[1] For my advocacy of preaching on whole biblical books, see my two volumes, *Preaching on the Books of the Old Testament* and *Preaching on the Books of the New Testament* (New York: Harper & Row, 1961 and 1956).

pared by the Christian Literature Commission.[2] This latter plan is based upon a systematic reading of the Bible at the rate of about one book per month. Some men keep a notebook or card file of texts that "leap at them" as they read and study the Bible; then from among these "live" scriptures they choose the passages to be used for sermons. Such a reservoir, held in reserve, saves the preacher from the shallow dipping of last-minute preparation.

In any case, the study of a passage which is to serve as the text of a single sermon on a given Sunday is best pursued against the background of a more comprehensive program of Bible study and in terms of a plan of Christian preaching which is undertaken in broad perspective. Some men will prefer to make detailed decisions about texts for a whole year in advance; others, after adopting an overall plan, will want to leave the choice of specific texts to the week preceding the sermon. In either case, and in all intermediate plans, what matters is that the choice of text is not left to caprice or abandoned to chance.

### Place the Text in Context

All textual preaching should be contextual. It should have as its horizon nothing less than the whole biblical world, as its purpose nothing less than the mind of Christ.

This means that work on a sermon will be informed in advance on Old Testament religion, New Testament theology, on the history of the Hebrew people, on the life of Jesus and the early church.

More immediately, the study of the text requires a reading knowledge and study of the biblical book of which it is a part. The questions raised by the disciplines of higher criticism should be asked and answered, with the help of good commentaries: Who wrote the book? To whom? When? Under what

[2] Box 179, St. Louis, Mo.   63166.

circumstances? Why did he write it? What was the burden of his message, seen as a unity? The struggle to answer these questions on one's own from his own firsthand reading of the book may well precede, but should always be followed and corrected by, the reading of established biblical scholars.

The biblical preacher will need a good outline of the biblical book from which his text is taken. He may devise this outline himself from his own study of the book, or he may have recourse to the outline of another.[3]

It is always helpful to place the text in context within the next subdivision of the book to which it belongs. For example, suppose that your text is I Cor. 13. The subunit to which this chapter belongs is Paul's discourse on the use of spiritual gifts, which includes three chapters—12, 13, and 14. These three chapters should be read as a unit.

To get one's final bearing on the passage, it is always helpful to test the passage itself and one's understanding of it by looking to the center of the whole biblical drama—God in Christ reconciling the world to himself. The ultimate light of meaning always depends upon that.

### Spell Out the Meaning of the Text

This is the work of exegesis. It may well begin by determining the type of literature to which the text belongs. Is it prophecy, gospel, epistle, apocalyptic, or what? Then one should go on to grasp the special hermeneutical principles which control the interpretation of that type of literature. Part II of the present volume will pay particular attention to these, chapter by chapter. At the moment, a brief sample will suffice.

A parable should be studied as a tale designed to make a single point. An allegory, in contrast, "walks on all fours"—it

---

[3] I have undertaken to provide an outline for every book of the Bible in my two books referred to in footnote 1 in this chapter.

has many meanings. A miracle is best interpreted as an acted parable—it too makes a single point. Hebrew poetry, written in parallelism, frequently expresses the same idea twice using different words. To cite an instance, consider Matthew's use of Zech. 9:9, which is Hebrew poetry written in synonymous parallelism:

> Rejoice greatly, O daughter of Zion!
>   Shout aloud, O daughter of Jerusalem!
> Lo, your king comes to you;
>   triumphant and victorious is he,
> humble and riding on an ass,
>   on a colt the foal of an ass.

In this poem, Zion and Jerusalem are synonymous—one city, not two different ones. And in the same way, the "ass" and "a colt the foal of an ass" are synonymous—a single animal, not two different ones. In the use of this passage, both Luke and Mark cause the disciples to acquire only one animal for the triumphal entry; but Matthew, misreading the parallelism to mean two animals, requires two animals—an ass and a colt. The resultant picture in Matt. 21:7 is somewhat awkward, to say the least!

To continue the discussion of special hermeneutical principles for the interpretation of particular types of literature, it is appropriate to say a word about the understanding of biblical personalities. It is only natural to try to turn a biblical person into a hero to be emulated. Closer scrutiny, however, will show us that all persons within the Bible, save one, have flaws and at some point come under the judgment of God. Only God is good, as Jesus himself said. This should teach us to center our attention not upon the biblical person, but rather upon the relationship of that person to God: his rebellion or reluctance, his acceptance or rejection of his call, and his personal growth in relation to crises, turnings, and ultimate surrender.

Every biblical text is part of a literature and as such falls under the canons of a particular literary type. These canons must be known and applied, else meaning is distorted.

After literary canons have been applied, there is always the task of translating out of the original tongues. With the help of good modern versions most of this work is already done. To deprive oneself of this help would be foolish. It would seem logical that a biblical preacher should have several of these versions in his library within arm's reach of his desk and that he would make it a regular practice to read his text each week in at least three of them. Sometimes there is unexpected impact in a particular rendition of a passage. For example, Matt. 21:13 in the RSV, reporting the cleansing of the temple, reads: "It is written, 'My house shall be called a house of prayer'; but you make it a den of robbers." One thinks at once of Jeremiah's temple sermon, reflected here. In the Anchor Bible, "den of robbers" takes on a keener edge in Jer. 7:11. "A robber's hide-out—is that what this house, which bears my name, has become in your opinion?" "A robber's hide-out" is much more striking than "a den of robbers." It illumines a whole new dimension of meaning; and it all comes from looking into a new translation into modern English.

Next comes the phrase-by-phrase, word-by-word study of the text, using good commentaries and the original languages, Hebrew and Greek, if possible. It helps, for instance, to know that the Greek word translated "desolate" in the RSV of John 14:18 is "orphanous," which quite literally means "orphans." The meaning stands up bold and clear: "I will not leave you as orphans; I will come to you." There can be no substitute for careful exegesis.

## 4 Put Yourself into the Text

Perhaps it should be said differently: Place your life as a Christian man before the text. We are here responding to the fact that the Bible is a book of faith and that it is read on its own plane only in terms of the confrontations of faith. Through it God makes a claim upon the life of the reader. It is a personal word which can be received in its depths only in personal terms. Again to quote Rudolf Bultmann, "The hearing of the word of the Bible can take place only in personal decision." Without the response of faith—as surrender and trust, not merely as belief—a man may stand full in the blazing light of revelation and yet see nothing.

It is here assumed that no man can preach movingly on any text as long as he is using that text solely as a channel of revelation to other men. He cannot speak on behalf of God to another until he himself has listened to God. In fact, all the speech of the pulpit should have its fundamental orientation not in the gifts of eloquence but in the disciplines of listening and responding to the speech of God addressed personally to the preacher. No man can properly preach on a biblical passage until he himself has listened to God speak to him personally through that passage. Otherwise the preacher will use the text not as a key to open lives to God, but as a weapon with which to bludgeon them.

To ascertain the point of personal involvement, one must first approach the passage as the record of a past event in its original setting. It is helpful to ask, "What was the original God-man encounter disclosed within this passage? What was the dialogue?" This is different from the questions of higher criticism only in its personal dimension. It looks through the passage to the divine-human encounter; it looks for the meeting of God with flesh-and-blood men in times past; it studies biblical events and sayings not for things in themselves, but for ultimate relationships on the personal plane.

Once the question of the past dialogue of God and man has been raised and answered, it is possible to ask, "Where do I enter the conversation? What is the dialogue between God and me to which this passage points?" When one has reached this stage of biblical study he has moved from the shallow knower-object relationship in which he interprets the text to a deeper level of I-Thou relationship in which the text interprets him.

The personal confrontation for which I am contending presupposes but outstrips all academic disciplines. It is an indispensable requisite to the personal interpretation of scripture upon which preaching depends. For that matter, it is also an indispensable requisite to the private reading of the Bible as a book of faith.

### Seek the Internal Unity of the Text

When one has a text of traditionally short length—only a verse or two—the problem of unity is relatively simple. But when one begins to deal with larger units of scripture, as advocated in this book, discovering the unity of the text and maintaining unity in the sermon become more difficult; also more crucial. Unless specific attention is given to this aspect of the passage, the text may be fragmented and the sermon built upon it may fly away into incoherence and riot.

As an aid to the discovery of the internal unity of a passage, one may profitably write out three things: (1) the proposition or theme, (2) the aim, and (3) a key verse, if there is one. By *proposition* is meant the theme of the passage when it is boiled down to a simple declarative statement containing a subject and a predicate. In a textual sermon the proposition of the passage also becomes the proposition of the sermon. By *aim* we mean

68

not the subject but the object of the passage—what it is trying to accomplish, why it was written. Again, in a textual sermon the aim of the passage becomes the aim of the sermon. A *key verse* of scripture, when it exists, has the virtue of stating the proposition of the passage and of the sermon in the language of scripture; it may also be used symphonically in the actual delivery of the sermon as a shorter form of the text. Like the North Star, it will keep calling the wandering preacher back to his true course.

## Uncover the Dynamics of the Text

The discovery of the inner dynamics of a scriptural passage is more than a search for structural outline. It is a probing for the movement, the development that takes place there. Outline and structure suggest something static and impersonal. Dynamics suggests the movement and life out of which the passage came and which it may re-create.

When seeking the surging life of a passage in this way, one has few guideposts; the life of a passage creates its own criteria. Nevertheless there are some questions which one may put to a passage that may be helpful: *What is the creative tension that one finds here?* What is at issue? Is there a conflict? If so, is it within a man, between men, or between man and God? What decision is called for? *What is the movement that occurs here?* Besides the movement of time and space there may be change of attitudes, deepening of understanding, progress or regress of character. As a reflection of the life upon which it reports and which it calls into being, the passage is living, therefore moving and growing. *Is there a climax?* At what point does the movement of the passage arrive at a crisis—come to crucial issue? *What is the outcome?* Sometimes the outcome is not stated but is left up to the hearer, as in the parable of the prodigal son, in which the elder brother remains on the outside debating whether he will enter to greet his brother and welcome him back home. The desired outcome for the elder brother and his counterpart, the pharisaic listener, is perfectly obvious.

## 7 Write a Précis of the Text

A *précis* (pray'-see) is a brief summary in the form of a paraphrase. It maintains the original standpoint of the text but aims to present its content within a smaller compass. This act of writing out the meaning of the passage in one's own words is singularly rewarding. It is a step beyond the reading of good paraphrases and careful work with commentaries and lexicons. It has a way of internalizing the message, of bringing it home to the student in his own terms. As such, it is excellent preparation for preaching.

The seven steps just outlined are hermeneutical, as distinguished from homiletical. They are foundational to the work of sermon-making and they must precede it. They constitute the task of the preacher as a biblical *student* who, for the time being, has kept the maker of sermons waiting in the outer office. When that task is done, and only then, should he permit himself to open the door and invite the minister as *preacher* to come in.

# 5

## The Minister as a Biblical Preacher

What has been said so far is addressed to the minister as student; it has to do with his hermeneutical skills and disciplines. The present chapter turns to homiletical skills and disciplines. It concerns the minister in the preparation of his sermons.

### False Approaches

As the body of scripture dealt with in a sermon increases beyond a verse or two, the difficulty of keeping the discourse within bounds as a true sermon increases. The minister as preacher needs to be on guard against several false approaches.

*It must not be assumed that biblical preaching is merely preaching that contains a great deal of scripture.* An evangelist of whom I heard recently includes a guarantee in his promotional literature: "Guaranteed, at least forty-five biblical quotations in every sermon." One suspects that these quotations were drawn from the Bible as though it were an arsenal and deployed as though they were weapons. In any case, the biblical character of a sermon is not determined by the amount of scripture used. A single text may be so used as to be in reality nothing more than a pretext or motto; it may not really guide the thought of the sermon at all. Texts, long or short, may be used as proof texts, in which case they are a homiletical attempt to take the

71

kingdom of God by violence. Sermons on biblical passages may never have emerged from the preliminary stage of biblical study, so that they turn out to be nothing more than biblical lectures. Things are not always what they seem; sermons purporting to be biblical and having many outward marks may not be biblical at all. The mere presence of scripture does not make them so.

*Biblical preaching is never antiquarian.* It draws on the ancient past, to be sure, but the sound of the sermon is never merely an echo in a museum. It rings with contemporaneity. Even when the sermon dwells upon the past it does so in living terms, so that the timeless and the timely shine through. Ralph W. Sockman once began a sermon on the prophet Amos in words like these: "Amos, the rustic, went up to the big city." He was speaking to a Park Avenue audience. He was talking about a Palestinian farmer who lived and died 2,600 years ago. But he was at the same time talking to and about most of his hearers who had come up from the small towns and the farms of America to look for their fortune in metropolitan New York. "You can get the hick out of the country; but you can't get the country out of the hick." This remark, in the manner of an Artemus Ward or Mark Twain, states the psychological situation which binds the sophisticated New Yorker to the simple Judean peasant, though an ocean of time seems to separate them. Sockman had drawn upon that common psychological experience to bind ancient and modern into a living unity.

For the same reason the sermonic habit of yesteryear, separating exposition and application, is also to be resisted. It is probably a defect in twentieth-century Americans that they are so biased against history. Not all people have felt this way about the past. But defect or not, it is a fact about the modern man which makes him impatient with a sermon that dwells for ten or fifteen minutes on Moses or Paul and only for the last five minutes upon him and his contemporaries. By the time the modern application appears in such a sermon, he will have absented himself "to think about something pleasant." Besides, ancient and modern words, when taken as witnesses to the ever-living God, are not properly divided into past and present in the ordinary sense. The ancient event and the ever new life of the spirit, as John Knox phrased them, are fundamentally united in the contemporaneity of God.

Jean-Jacques von Allmen, in a penetrating study on *Preaching and Congregation,* comments upon this very point:

> The duty of preaching, at God's own command, is to translate this Word into languages other than Aramaic, and to make it present to generations other than the first of the Christian era. Obviously the translation spoken of here involves more than mere recourse to dictionaries and grammars, and making the Word present requires more than a glance at the calendar. Preaching is thus an enormous power for unity, since it binds all tongues (that is to say all nations) and all ages to the central event of history. In bringing together God's people, preaching really brings together the whole world in order to point it towards its Saviour and its Lord Jesus Christ. It serves Him in whom God sums up all things. (Eph. 1:10) .[1]

There is a third false approach to guard against. *A biblical sermon must not submerge the main point of a passage under an avalanche of detail.* When using a body of scripture larger than a traditional text of one or two verses, it is possible to lose the sermon in discursiveness. There are interesting but marginal matters which invite a detour of the attention from the main business of the text. But even when the central point is not lost in such distraction, it is possible to obscure it under a burden of

[1] (Richmond: John Knox Press, 1962) , p. 23.

detail. Obscuring detail may overwhelm a sermon in one or both of two ways: in its matter or in its structure.

As to matter, the shape of a passage may be lost in excessive attention to detail. It may be smothered in minutiae, choked to death by the pedantry of the preacher. For instance, a sermon on the commandment, "Thou shalt not steal," cannot go minutely into the distinctions between theft and robbery or dwell upon the penalties for such to be found in the Law of Moses. Or a biographical sermon on Jeremiah cannot rehearse every event of his life told in the book from his call to his captivity. Selectivity and restraint must be exercised in choosing only those supporting details, those events and quotations, which illustrate the proposition and sharpen the aim of the passage.

As to structure, a passage must not be allowed to break down into a verse-by-verse commentary. A sermon on the Lord's Prayer should not merely take up that prayer petition by petition. As a rule, a sermon requires a simplifying outline of not more than five main points. Consider one possible outline of the Lord's Prayer (Matt. 6:9-13) :

I. The address to God
   A. As universal Father: "Our Father"
   B. As transcendent and sovereign: "Who art in heaven"
   C. As worthy of all praise: "Hallowed be thy name."
II. A petition for God's reign over all men: "Thy kingdom come, thy will be done, on earth as it is in heaven."
III. A prayer for ourselves
   A. For our physical needs: "Give us this day our daily bread."
   B. For our spiritual healing: "And forgive us our debts, as we also have forgiven our debtors."
   C. For our spiritual safety: "And lead us not into temptation, but deliver us from evil."

Consider a fourth false approach. *A biblical sermon must be more than a research product.* At one extreme, if it relies on research alone, it may be competently but coldly intellectual. At the other, it may be a "scissors and paste" montage of quotations from commentaries, anthologies, and books of illustration —a retailing of other men's thoughts.

A sermon is not so much made as grown, not so much built as received. The ideas of a sermon must be given time to sink deep into the emotions of the preacher and then to rise organically out of his whole life, enriched by memory, fired by conviction. The text must be given time to play like a searchlight over the faces of the congregation, illuminating the shadowed places in the lives under the care of their preacher who is also their pastor. And, beyond that, the text must be set in dialogue with contemporary culture in all the concreteness and paradox of its current manifestations. This means that no preacher can do his task of preparing biblical sermons as a mere technician, however disciplined. He will need the deeper and more subtle disciplines of the creative artist.

## Creative Homiletics

After the study of a text has been brought through the steps suggested in chapter 4, it is ready for the distinctively homiletical work which will present it in a sermon.

There is much that remains to be done. The preacher himself must live his way into the text. He must search for and find concrete points of personal involvement—his own and his hearers'—and specific instances of contemporary relevance. He must present the ideas of the text imaginatively—in analogies, similes, metaphors, and by way of anecdote and example. The whole matter must be brought down the abstraction ladder to solid earth and given a habitation. The sermon must be named. And given an outline. Then written out or spoken out in full, phrase by phrase, sentence by sentence.

For true preaching, none of this can be done mechanically. It requires a way of working that takes advantage of the processes used—wittingly or unwittingly—by poets, painters, sculptors, novelists, playwrights, composers, and scientists (insofar as they are more than technicians). In recent years these processes have been systematically studied and analyzed by a number of scholars and presented in several distinguished and helpful volumes.

The exact scheme evolved in each study is categorized in slightly different ways, but all agree basically. For convenience' sake, I will adopt the scheme of Eliot D. Hutchinson. He diagrams it as follows: [2]

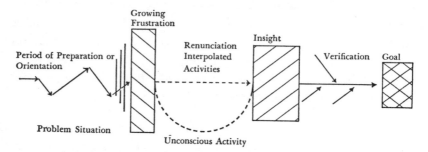

Given urgent concern and hard work in the period of *preparation,* plus time to let incubation take place during the period of *renunciation,* the unconscious mind will become a resourceful ally, thrusting up into the conscious mind its gifts of illumination or *insight.* The agony and ecstasy of such creative thought are faithfully mirrored in the words of the psalmist:

> I was dumb and silent,
>   I held my peace to no avail;
> my distress grew worse,
>   my heart became hot within me.

[2] "Interrelation of Phases in the Process of Insight," adapted from Eliot D. Hutchinson, *How to Think Creatively* (Nashville: Abingdon, 1949), p. 41.

*As I mused, the fire burned;* [3]
then I spoke with my tongue. (Ps. 39:2-3.)

Every minister confronted with the necessity of presenting a new sermon every Sunday knows the distress described in these verses. He goes through the weekly agony of searching for an idea, or, given the idea, he goes through the agony of growing that idea into a full sermon. It is this distress, however—this agony—which seems to alert the basement workshop of the brain and set the unconscious mind to work. In a word, it is the agony and distress of the period of preparation that make the ecstasy of insight possible. Any minister who may have robbed himself of such ecstasy by a too mechanical approach to sermon construction has missed one of the supreme joys of living. This begetting of ideas, this birth of insight, is akin to the awe and wonder of biological parenthood. But, more important, it marks the difference between a sermon off the top of the mind and one which has its roots deep down in memory and emotion, nourished by the whole life of the preacher.

Let us turn now to the task of putting these processes of creative insight to work in the growth of a biblical sermon. The hard work of biblical study already expended upon the text will probably have been, in its own right, a period of preparation encountering many frustrations. Such a study may have extended over several days, in which case there was a period of renunciation during which incubation could and probably did take place. The result may very well have been a sudden, leaping flame of insight at some point in the study, especially as that study was concerned to find the unity of the passage in a single proposition and to discover the single target of purpose to be found

---

[3] Italics mine. Though not addressed to a speech situation, these words faithfully mirror the process of creative thought. In this instance the psalmist's first inclination toward vengeance was transmuted into prayer.

within it. If such insight has already come, it now takes on the character of initial insight of or insight as partial solution, and stands at the beginning of a whole new cycle of endeavor in search of the final form and content of the sermon. This new cycle repeats the pattern: preparation, growing frustration, renunciation, insight; then it goes on to the arduous task of verification (outlining and writing) until the goal in the form of the completed sermon is achieved.

*The stage of preparation.* The hard, consecutive study and logical thought given to the task up until this point needs now to be suspended in the interest of free association. Holding the text in mind, especially as grasped at center in its proposition and aim, let it become the magnet attracting everything that is drawn to it in the free play of imagination. The mind is open; it will accept all suggestions at this stage, reject none. It now indulges in the chaotic prologue to the dawn of creation, when the world is without form and void, and darkness broods upon the face of the deep (Gen. 1:2). Variously called "brainstorming," "yeasting," or "brooding," this is the "musing" of Ps. 39:3 which is prerequisite to everything else in the process.

In the early stages deliberately resist the temptation to devise an outline for the sermon. Achieved too early, the outline tends to stifle imagination; the result may be a well-structured sermon as bare as a skeleton. Search, instead, for the content of the sermon, the living material relating it to sight and sound, touch, taste, smell, and motor sensations of flesh-and-blood involvement experienced, seen, remembered, and imagined in the life of the preacher and his associates. Everything the preacher has known, experienced, done, said, heard, and read becomes a deep artesian well for the living water of this sermon. Let it flow.

Let it flow until it dwindles to a trickle, then stops. That is, until frustration is experienced and resisted to the point of exhaustion. Then renounce it; give it up for a while. Sleep on it. Let the period of incubation set in. In a word, send it downstairs to the basement workshop of the mind. Return to it next day and continue brooding day after day until there is a breakthrough.

Periods of conscious preparation, in the manner of free association just described, will normally last from half an hour to forty-five minutes per day, though they may last longer. Many ministers, to keep their minds on the track, find it useful to make penciled notes on "brooding sheets." Entered helter-skelter, these jottings of disconnected words and phrases clutter the page, making sense to no one but their author; but they seem to have the power to keep him at it and even serve as a catalytic agent, hastening the process. They also have the virtue of retaining the broodings for the next day.

*The stage of renunciation and incubation.* The basement workshop of the mind is now humming. While you are sleeping, driving, walking, listening to music, doing routine tasks, or talking with friends, the unconscious mind will be working away. Now and then it will make itself known as it seizes upon an incident or phrase from the field of conscious attention. It may send up signals of progress to be entered casually on the backs of envelopes or scraps of paper or cards and retained for the next conscious period of brooding. The stage of incubation may be an uneasy time—a period of gestation—commingling expectancy and anxiety, eagerness and irritation contributing to stretches of absentmindedness and preoccupation apt to be annoying to wives, children, and intimate friends. This is a time of creative waiting, in which the gift of insight is being formed.

*The stage of insight or illumination.* Then, eureka! It comes! It comes as a flash, in a moment of time. Frequently this flash of insight is preceded by an intimation that the problem has

79

solved itself at the back of the mind and that the solution is about to come forth. Often the insight is triggered into awareness by an accidental occasion—as the swinging lamps in the Cathedral of Pisa may have triggered the law of the pendulum in the mind of Galileo, or as the herd of hippopotamuses swimming in the Congo River triggered Albert Schweitzer's central life principle, "reverence for life." [4]

Sometimes the whole plan of a sermon opens at the time of insight. In any case, the way to outline now opens up and its time is ripe.

Emotionally, the time of insight is one of great release and happiness. It is the ecstasy which answers to the agony of the preliminary stages. And it is also the thrust behind the work that remains to be done.

*The stage of verification.* This label is more appropriate to a hypothesis of science than to a poem, a play, or a sermon. As applied to the sermon, this is the time of detailed outlining, the time for the selecting and excluding of material, the time for exact phrasing and wording. It is also the time for double-checking and verifying quotations, facts, and incidents drawn from the general body of knowledge. It is the time when the fruitful chaos of creation is ordered into a structured world. The work of this stage contains a good deal of drudgery and may, again, proceed only against emotional resistance; but it is necessary.

---

[4] For an extended example of the application of the principles of creative thinking to the evolving of Schweitzer's *philosophy of civilization,* worked out over a period of more than fifty years, see his book *Out of My Life and Thought* tr. by C. T. Campion (New York: Henry Holt & Co., 1933), pp. 172-90. The processes are the same as those for a sermon, though the tempo is greatly altered for the longer, more difficult work resulting in three large volumes of original philosophy. It is a testimony to the creative genius of Schweitzer that he could endure for half a century the frustrations of gestating thought which plague a minister for two or three days.

In doing this work, the minister will be well advised to work in cooperation with his own best endowments. Some men find it more satisfactory to prepare on paper, outlining in detail, then write a full manuscript and revise that. Others like to prepare by an auditory method—talking the message out, stage by stage, until it has evolved into the sermon to be delivered on Sunday. Sometimes this is an inward talking—"subvocal articulation," as the Watsonian behaviorists used to label it. Sometimes it is talking out loud, in an empty auditorium or in the study itself; it may actually be delivered to a secretary or into a dictating machine or tape recorder. Some men pace up and down in their studies during such dictation, accompanying the movement of their minds with the motion of their bodies as a sort of stimulus to expression. In any case, the flash of insight has to be put to work; the sermon has to be outlined and articulated into actual sentences and paragraphs.

All this, in turn, becomes preparation and resource for the actual sermon itself, which is the sermon in the midst of the congregation at the creative moment of delivery. This final preparation to deliver, as distinguished from the preparation of the sermon, has its own demands and is worthy of a book in its own right. Limitations of space forbid our discussing them here.[5]

### Putting the Process to Work

How does all this work out in terms of a weekly schedule? Each man will find his own pace; but just to be as specific and as helpful as possible, let me suggest two possibilities which may be modified by the reader in various ways:

*Schedule Number One.* The preliminary biblical study

[5] For a book-length presentation of these factors see Dwight E. Stevenson and Charles F. Diehl, *Reaching People from the Pulpit* (New York: Harper & Row, 1958).

81

suggested in chapter 4 will have been brought to completion a week or ten days prior to the actual work of preparing the sermon. It will occupy its own time slot "across the board," a time slot adjacent to but not interfering with the time slot of the sermon in preparation for the Sunday just at hand. For example, for the sermon to be preached on Sunday, May 14, the Bible study will have been completed before Sunday, May 7. This will leave time for brooding and incubation from, say, Monday, May 8, through Wednesday or Thursday, May 9 or 10, in the expectation—to be tested by experience—that insight will come by Thursday or Friday, so that the sermon may be written or composed on Friday or Saturday, May 12 or 13, and preached on Sunday, May 14.

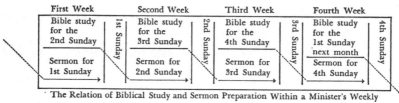

The Relation of Biblical Study and Sermon Preparation Within a Minister's Weekly Study Schedule—Plan No. 1

*Schedule Number Two.* The whole plan is telescoped into a single week. The first two days—hardly more can be allowed—will be given to the intensive study of the text in the manner of chapter 4 in this book. The brooding will have been dovetailed into this study to some extent but will take free play not later than Wednesday, when the normal pattern of creative thought will unfold, phase by phase. This is for "the quick study," the mind that moves at a swifter pace.

Which plan, or modification thereof, is to be followed will have to be determined by the trial and error of experiment. Whatever plan is adopted, one thing is clear: If the resources of creativity are to be utilized, the preparation of the sermon must be spread over several days. It may not be postponed, then desperately rammed into the lamplit hours of Saturday night— not if the preacher is to have the unconscious mind as an ally.

## Some Clues for Hastening Insight

Arthur Koestler in a monumental study, *The Act of Creation*, has shown that insight occurs when two dissociated planes of life or thought intersect—become bisociated. Galileo's law of the pendulum, for example, came to him when the plane of church liturgy and architecture intersected the plane of mathematical and physical science; and Galileo saw the swinging ornate ecclesiastical lamp in the cathedral not as a lamp at all, but as a pendulum.

A sermon on "The Sense of Belonging" came into being one morning at five o'clock on a pullman sleeper in this manner: The minister had been struggling all week with the problem of what to say to a town-gown congregation on the first Sunday after the opening of college in a year when a Navy V-12 unit occupied the girls' dormitories, the girls had been moved into men's fraternity houses, and civilian men had been crowded into private homes. In a word, everybody in that small college town had been pressed into a serious game of "fruit basket upset," and everyone was a stranger there during that week—both those who had just arrived and those who had lived there for years. The situation was a unique one; it unified the whole community, and the minister felt that it was imperative that he address himself to it. But the sermon would not come. Neither text nor idea presented itself.

He was at that stage of frustration when he was called away for a denominational meeting in another city requiring a trip

83

to and from the meeting by overnight train. Pulling back into his own city after the meeting, he was sitting in the lounge car at five o'clock in the morning. The only other occupant was a sleepy GI, who, in the dawn's early light, looked out upon the unfamiliar mountainous landscape with obvious distaste, and who, when he could contain his disgust no longer, blurted out, "What a godforsaken place this is!"

The minister, secretly offended at the GI's dislike of a landscape that he himself loved, countered immediately with a question, "Where are *you* from?"

The reply came in a slow drawl, the regional speech of the great, wide-open Southwest: "Texas." The American GI felt no sense of belonging here in a hilly setting where the minister was happily at home. In that moment there flashed into the mind of the preacher the whole secret of Sunday's sermon, in the form of title and text: "The Sense of Belonging" from I Cor. 3:21-23, "For all things are yours, whether Paul or Apollos or Cephas or the world or life or death or the present or the future, all are yours; and you are Christ's; and Christ is God's." Thereafter the sermon almost prepared itself.

In this example it should be noted that two planes of experience, normally separated, momentarily intersected. Insight resulted. It should also be noted that the conversation with the soldier was an *accidental occasion* which served to trigger the insight. The minister was responsive to it only because he had struggled in some distress and anxiety with the situation to which he felt constrained to preach the following Sunday—a situation in which the sense of belonging of every member of his congregation had been disturbed, but which he had so far been unable to put into words.

The clue to be gained from all this is that the brooding period and the period of incubation to follow are times during which the creative thinker must be ready to see things in new perspectives and in unexpected relationships. Mentally, he must stand on his head, as it were, or look on the world through his legs, or tilt his head and see the world obliquely. It is helpful to raise such questions as: Suppose it were not so, how else could it be? Why does it have to be this way; why not exactly opposite? How would this look from the pew, rather than from the pulpit? What is the trouble here?

Recently a minister was struggling with the text from Col. 1:17, "He is before all things, and in him [Christ] all things hold together." Pondering this text, he said to himself, "Suppose things did not hold together; suppose everything came unglued at the joints; what kind of world would we have?" He had recently been reading some plays of the avant-garde theatre, Eugene Ionesco's *Bald Soprano* among them. In this play the clock chimed at random when it pleased and as many times as it pleased—the expected sequence of ordered time was demolished. The title had nothing to do with the play. In fact, nothing in the play had much to do with anything else. Conversation was nonsense. Logic had vanished. Lifelong associations provided no bridge of memory or love; communication had broken down. People could not really talk to each other. Their world had come unglued; in no one and in nothing did things hold together for them. This is a bold, negative way of calling attention to the concrete reality of spiritual community, in which language can be used to convey truth in spite of some falsehood, reason can operate with some assurance that unreason will not unseat it, and bonds of memory and love can bind human beings to each other in spite of some misunderstandings and some friction between them. In any kind of life that has not come unglued at the joints, there must be some cosmic principle of coherence, some integrating power, some spiritual presence. The minister had his sermon. The living Christ is that integrating spiritual presence, the concrete reality of God's love: "In him all things hold together." An Ionesco play and a text from the apostle Paul do not on the surface suggest each other, but when they are brought together, they intersect, yielding the insight of a sermon.

Imagination, as just illustrated, is simply the capacity to see old and familiar things in new associations from new perspectives, to combine things not previously put together. It is possible to put oneself in an imaginative frame of mind deliberately and thus to spread the net of creative expectancy in which new insights are caught.

Beyond this, two other things may contribute to the hastening of insight. One is the intensification of the stage of preparation —taking the problem seriously, really struggling with it from a sense of urgency and importance for the final outcome. A man who sees his sermon as idle chatter accomplishing nothing will discover little creativity in sermon preparation. But the man who sees his sermons as words of redemption, dividing life and death for at least some of his hearers, will approach his work of preparation with the motivations out of which creative words can rise. Intensify the period of preparation; increase the urgency of your motivation; and you will hasten creativity.

The second additional thing that will hasten insight is the reinforcement of habit. Work at the task of sermon preparation at a regular series of times, in a regular place, and through regular routines. These reinforcements from habit will serve, in turn, to intensify the period of preparation and to increase expectancy, and thus to provide the atmosphere in which insight may be stimulated, then recognized and welcomed when it comes.

The minister will do his best work as a biblical preacher when he approaches his preparation in two stages—first as biblical student, second as biblical preacher. He should keep these stages separate and in proper sequence, working industriously at both. Given these, it is hardly conceivable that he will not bound forward in his development as a relevant and helpful servant of the Word.

# Part II

# PRODUCTION

# 6

## Preaching on a Biblical Personality

Biographical sermons on biblical personalities are popular, both with ministers and with laymen. Besides, the Bible itself predisposes us toward such a treatment of its content; men and women swarm through its pages. Its lessons are never stated in terms of abstract principles, but instead are bodied forth in the flesh and blood of fully human, all too human people. Preaching that deals centrally with persons is close to the Bible's own way of looking at religion. It is startling and instructive to discover that the book of Acts has a human cast of no less than 110 people! The human network of Paul, which one meets in the opening and concluding verses of his letters, is a numerous company. The Gospels teem with humanity—met as multitudes, small groups, and individuals. As for the Old Testament, from its pages march the very hosts of Israel: patriarchs, kings, commoners, prophets, priests, sages, generals, renegades, and villains. A bare census of the human population of the Bible would result in a directory of names as numerous as the inhabitants of a modern city. What is more, it would give us a veritable cross-section of universal humanity.

The present chapter will be a case study in preparing to

preach on a biblical personality, using the patriarch Jacob as its subject. Jacob has been chosen both for his importance and for the fact that his story runs through several chapters of a biblical book, and, consequently, taxes a minister's powers of compression and unity. If one can prepare a sermon from a biography that extensive, he will have no difficulty with the shorter narratives.

## Interpreting Biblical Biographies

In approaching the patriarch Jacob, as with any personality in scripture, there are some special guidelines to follow.

(1) *Biblical biography is not biography in the modern sense.* It has no interest in telling the story of a human life merely to satisfy curiosity or to supply a knowledge of biographical incidents as such. Personal narrative is a part of the larger narrative of scripture, which is sacred history, *Heilsgeschichte,* the history of salvation. As such, it is revelatory. It casts light upon the ways of God with men and of men with God; and, even more important, it draws men toward God. It is purposeful narrative and may properly be analyzed for its purpose.

(2) *Biblical personalities are not presented as ideal heroes to be imitated.* In biblical thought, only God and his Son are completely good. All human beings are in some respects imperfect, if not downright pernicious. In giving us the portrait of a man, the Bible is candid camera photography; it gives us everything, warts and blemishes included. Though it does not dwell on the sordid side, neither does it neglect it nor gloss over it. Biblical literature is realistic. Its picture of human nature is honest, geared neither to flattery nor to emulation.

(3) *The reader's attention should be centered not upon the biblical person in isolation, but upon his relationships—primarily to God, but secondarily and also to his fellows.* It is in

the space between men and God that the action takes place. In fact, a good man-made title for the Bible might be *Between Men and God*. Focused upon relationships, the attention of the Bible student will be alert to the subject's rebellion or reluctance in answering God's call, upon his personal growth or decline in relation to God's claim upon him, upon conflicts, crises, turnings, capitulations, and consummations.

(4) Just as a biblical person must be set into relationships with God and his fellows, *so he also needs to be set within his times and related to his own culture and mores*. Do not expect Christian conduct of Joshua at the sack of Jericho! Try to understand the social customs forming the spiritual climate of his world. Every man, even a biblical man, is the child of his times. His ethics and insights need to be seen contextually.

(5) *The student of biblical biography should remember that some of the early personalities are eponymous; they are presented not only as individuals but also as personifications of whole peoples*. This is true especially of the patriarchal period. Thus, Esau is not only the son of Isaac, an individual; he is also Edom, the nation occupying Mount Seir, southeast of the Dead Sea. Jacob is Jacob; but he is also Israel in its genesis as a people. In studying such eponymous persons it is necessary to view them bifocally—now through one lens, then through the other.

(6) *To be seen properly, a biblical person must come to life before the eyes of the reader*. He will do this, often, if the reader will take the trouble to look among his acquaintances—and in his own household—for the biblical person's modern counterpart. The Bible is not a portrait gallery; it is a hall of mirrors. Look into it properly and you will see yourself, and all the other people that you associate with daily. This may be easier to do for the Old Testament than for the New on the whole, and

93

easier for some Old Testament figures than for others. There is more sense of identity with Jacob than with Paul; more with Jeremiah than with Moses; more with Peter than with James the brother of Jesus. Nevertheless, some measure of psychological identity between ourselves and the persons mirrored in the Bible will enable us to get under their skin and see things through their eyes. It is a worthwhile undertaking in the struggle for understanding, and scripture invites it.

(7) *A studious approach to any biblical personality will require comprehensive, sequential reading of the entire narrative about him, however widely it may be scattered through scripture.* But for this task there is excellent help available. In the four volumes of *The Interpreter's Dictionary of the Bible,* as in the briefer *Harper's Bible Dictionary* and *Hastings' Dictionary of the Bible* (recently revised), there are reliable scholarly summaries, replete with all biblical references. It is always useful to read such summaries, especially in the newer dictionaries which reflect the latest conclusions of biblical scholarship.

## The Text

The narrative of Jacob occupies about a third of the book of Genesis. It is found in Gen. 25:21-34; plus chapters 27–35 and 37–50. The last section, chapters 37–50, is principally the story of Joseph; but the story of Jacob is intimately intertwined with that of Joseph, and in a unique way is brought to climax and fulfillment in Joseph.

An episodic listing of the narrative runs as follows: The birth of Jacob and his twin brother, Esau (Gen. 25:19-26); Jacob filches Esau's birthright (25:27-34); Jacob steals the rightful blessing belonging to Esau (27:1-40); and earns Esau's hatred (27:41-45); Jacob flees from Esau's wrath (27:46–28:5); has a vision at Bethel (28:10-22); he journeys on to Paddan-aram, where he meets Rachel (29:1-14) ; marries and rears a family including eleven sons (29:15-35; 30:1-24) ; makes himself wealthy by outwitting his father-in-law, Laban (30:25-43) ; flees from Laban, setting out for Canaan (31:1-55) ; as he approaches Canaan, he prepares in great fear to meet his brother Esau, now become a mighty warlord (32:1-23) ; he wrestles with an invisible antagonist all through the night at the river Jabbok (32:24-32) ; and the next day meets Esau, with whom, surprisingly, he is reconciled (33:1-16) ; he then moves to Shechem (33:18-20), where his family collides with that of Hamor the Hivite (34:1-31) ; he next returns to Bethel (35:1-15) ; begets Benjamin (35:16-20) and conducts the life of his jealous sons (35:22b-26) ; he returns to Beer-sheba, where his father Isaac dies (35:27-29) ; is grief-stricken when Joseph, whom he thinks dead, is sold into slavery in Egypt (37:29-36) ; sends his sons to Egypt to buy grain during a famine (42:1-6) ; reluctantly allows Benjamin, the youngest and dearest son, to go along on the second trip for grain (43:1-15) ; with his whole family, is reunited with Joseph in Egypt (46:29-34), where they settle in Goshen (46:28–47:12) ; as he dies he gives his deathbed blessing to Joseph and speaks his final words to all his sons (47:27–49:28) ; he then dies and is buried in the family tomb at Hebron back in Canaan (49:29–50:13) .

## The Text in Context

The narrative of Jacob, the third of the patriarchs and the personification of early Israel, is told in the book of Genesis, which is presented as a kind of prologue to the main drama of the Bible. It shows the beginnings of the people of Israel and tells how they came to be enslaved in Egypt, where the main action of the drama of redemption begins. On the margins of this story there is much that has to do with the origin of shrines, rituals, customs, and tribes, and the relations of Israel to other peoples, especially the ancestral conflict of Israel and Edom. The setting is that of a pastoral and hunting economy; the life is that of nomads living in tents of goat's hair and moving from place to place in search of water and grasslands. The key theological concept is God's fashioning of a servant people and their election as a nation of priests through whom all the peoples of the world are to be blessed.

## Spelling Out Some Textual Meanings

*The name Jacob* (Gen. 25:26; 27:36) . There is some speculation that the name Jacob, etymologically, may have meant "may God protect," but since it contains the common name for "heel" and the verb "to grasp by the heel," the scripture itself follows the popular meaning, and Jacob becomes "the supplanter." [1]

*Birthright* (Gen. 25:32-33) . Though it was legal for Esau to sell his birthright, it was foolishly shortsighted of him to do so. The birthright of the firstborn son entitled him to a double share in the inheritance of his father (property rights) and also made him the next head of the clan (political rights) .

*Blessing* (Gen. 27:27) . The blessings of a dying man were thought to have supernatural power. They were binding; once uttered they could not be revoked, not even by the speaker.

*Bethel* (Gen. 28:19) . The literal meaning is "house of God." The geological formation of the place, formerly called Luz, was such as to suggest a ladder or ramp leading from earth to heaven and from heaven to earth. Today at the northern boundaries of

[1] *Jacob* in Hebrew is יַעֲקֹב. Heel is עָקֵב. Change only the vowel pointing and one gets several meanings: heel, one who takes by the heel, to go behind one's heel, i.e., to resort to trickery or deceit.

Israel one faces, similarly, "the ladders of Lebanon." In the thought of the ancient past, the ladder (ramp) of Bethel was a kind of superhighway for the angels of God who used it for their traffic to and from earth. Jacob unwittingly had slept in the middle of all this unseen traffic; and when he discovered his blunder he was terrified.

*Mandrakes* (Gen. 30:14). Moffatt translated, *love apples.* The fruit was thought to have magical power over the eater.

*Poplar and almond rods* (Gen. 30:37). More ancient magic.

*Teraphim* (Gen. 31:19, 30, 32, 33-35). Small household gods, symbolic of property ownership; they were equivalent to deeds of ownership. Laban's distress over their theft is understandable.

*Mizpah* (Gen. 31:49). Watchpost, like the boundary markers, narrow heaps of stones, used to this day to mark the boundaries of fields in Jordan. Jacob and Laban were drawing the line between them and calling on God to keep a watchful eye, each upon his enemy, because they did not trust each other. Not a very beneficial benediction!

*The name Israel* (Gen. 32:27-29). There are some Hebrew scholars who see the name as derived from the word for God and the verb "to rule," and who think it means "let God rule." God is the subject of the verb. In recording or transmission, Jacob has become the subject of the verb. And yet it is clear that Jacob had not subdued God, but rather that the opposite was the case. The same connotation is found in the Hebrew word for "prevailed," which, according to a Jewish rabbi whom I consulted, literally means "not killed." The consequent interpretation is that Jacob's new name, Israel, meant "Let God rule," for Jacob had daringly wrestled with God, and had not

97

been killed, an awesome experience calculated to revolutionize one's life! [2]

*Peniel* and *Penuel* (Gen. 32:30, 31). Two variants of the same root, meaning quite literally "the face of God." According to Israelite tradition, the sight of God's face would kill a man. Thus Moses was not permitted to look upon God's face, only upon his back.

## Putting Yourself into the Text

Jacob, the crafty competitor, is too much like us for our own comfort. It is not only the neurotic culture of our times that makes us competitive; it is more fundamentally our anxious egocentricity that pits us against others. To the extent that we are infected by the striving for status, the ambition for power, the thirst for public recognition and prestige, we identify ourselves as brothers under the skin to the Old Testament heel-catcher. We status seekers, pyramid climbers, and waste makers play the game by his rules. It is even possible to compete in virtues: "I'm being more humble than you are!" And even within the church and among ministers, the race for preferment is not unknown as men hunger for bigger churches with larger staffs and larger salaries, long for civic accolades, denominational office, and honorary academic degrees.

This competitive world of the natural (as against the spiritual) man is not without God. But when God comes into our scheming, competitive world, he invades it as a supernatural guest who is not quite welcome, though we are reluctant to admit this to ourselves, let alone to say it out loud. In this

---

[2] In Hebrew, Israel, ישראל, is a compound. The word for God is the suffix El, אל. The rest of the name may or may not be derived from the verb, Sharar, שרר.

awkward situation we try to make our adjustments, hoping to stave off the day when we will have to meet God in face-to-face combat. The truth is that God threatens to bring the whole competitive structure into tumbled ruins about our ears, and we, having no notion of what another kind of world would be like, postpone the awful day as long as possible by all the tricks of cleverness and appeasement at our command. Meantime, we know full well that although we may postpone the showdown, we cannot avoid it forever.

## Finding the Internal Unity of the Text

*The aim of the text.* Stated in terms of the ancient past, the aim might read something like this: To show how Jacob, a self-willed and crafty competitor, met his match in God and became Israel, the father of a people chosen by God as servants of redemption to the nations. Stated in timeless terms, applicable to us, the aim may sound something like this: To show how God may take a natural, competitive man and tame him for his own purposes.

*The proposition implicit in the text.* There are many different verbal formulations of the central theme of Jacob's narrative. The minister as a biblical student will find himself phrasing and rephrasing these as he searches for a simple, clarifying, and unifying statement. From among several wordings, I have chosen two, the first more complex, the second less so:

(1) The hard competitor, fighting everyone he meets for his own selfish gain, weaves the net which God uses to catch him and confront him; then as this man wrestles alone with conscience and with God, he finds his new and rightful role.

(2) To compete is to best oneself in the end and to meet face to face with the supreme antagonist, God himself; once life

99

is determined from a new center by that crucial encounter, we are new persons with a new sense of destiny.

## Uncovering the Dynamics of the Text

The narrative moves by a kind of rhythmic tension: conflict, flight, encounter; flight, conflict, flight, conflict, encounter, capitulation. For the way in which this rhythmic pattern unfolded in Jacob's case, see the next section.

## A Précis of the Text

No statement by another will serve a preacher as well as his own statement, the product of his own mental struggle. The following précis is offered only as an illustration of the sort of condensed paraphrase that one man has worked out:

Jacob was one of twins. He and Esau fought even before they were born, and when they were born, though Esau was first, Jacob had him by the heel trying to supplant him. Esau, father of Edom, was a hunter. Jacob was a shepherd. Coming home from a fruitless hunt hungry, Esau one day sold his birthright to Jacob for a meal. So Jacob did supplant Esau, then added insult to injury by getting his father Isaac's blessing as well. Esau swore to kill him.

Jacob fled toward northern Syria, giving the excuse that he was going to look for a wife from among his own kind of people. En route he stopped to sleep at Bethel, only to find, to his horror, that he had lain down in the middle of the supernatural highway carrying traffic between heaven and earth. In the morning he tried to make the most of this awkward development by erecting an altar and striking a bargain with God—worship and tithes for service rendered, the service being protection, peace, and prosperity for Jacob.

He then went on to Paddan-aram, met Rachel, fell in love,

and to pay the dowry to Laban, Rachel's father, worked seven years as a farmhand. But Laban tricked him and palmed off Leah, his elder daughter, on the wedding night. Being a single-minded man, Jacob fought back, doggedly working seven more years for Rachel. From these two wives and two concubines he sired twelve sons who, in turn, were the fathers of the twelve tribes of Israel.

While Jacob was still without property of his own, he acquired great possessions by tricking the trickster, Laban. Thereby he earned the hostility of Laban and had to flee with flocks and family to escape Laban's wrath.

Now Jacob found himself "between the devil and the deep blue sea"; to escape Laban's wrath, he fled back toward the twenty-year wrath of Esau, who had become a warlord with an efficient army. Jacob plotted bribery and appeasement, and shook with terror over the prospective meeting with Esau. His stratagems of competitive cleverness, it appeared, had become bankrupt. Now he stood in need not of a fair fight but of mercy and forgiveness.

In this extremity, having sent everyone on ahead, he wrestled alone through the night with God at the fords of the Jabbok; in the morning he came away limping and with a new name, Israel. He was no longer Jacob, the ruthless competitor; he was now Israel, the man who had wrestled with God.

Jacob's successive history was not one of worldly success, for among his sons he began to reap the harvest of rivalry and jealousy that he had sown. The crowning sorrow of his life was the loss of his beloved son, Joseph, whom the other sons had sold into slavery, meantime convincing Jacob that a wild beast had slain him. To this sorrow was added the affliction of famine, which in turn was the means by which Jacob came to Egypt, only to discover that Joseph, his son, far from being dead, was actually grand vizier of all Egypt. To his amazement,

Jacob now realized that God had been leading him like a blind mule. In his blessing of Joseph, Jacob said:

> The God before whom my fathers
> Abraham and Isaac walked,
> the God who has led me all my life
> long to this day (Gen. 48:15).

That is the story of how the Israelites came to be in Egypt, ready prey for the hostile pharaoh who enslaved them and put them to hard labor. All this is prologue to the drama of deliverance which appears in the first act under the name of Exodus, "the way out."

### Brainstorming the Text

The scribblings of a man brooding in free association upon a text read like nonsense. In what follows there is no attempt to present a facsimile of a brooding sheet, but only to select a few elements which may have been called to mind in the brooding process. To all outward appearances, the suggestions are chaotic; it is to be hoped that the chaos is creative.

Karen Horney, psychoanalyst, has a book *The Neurotic Personality of Our Times* in which, in part, she traces personality-destroying anxiety and neurosis to the excessive competitiveness of American culture. Neurosis and competitiveness are joined in casual linkage.

Thomas Hobbes, three hundred years ago, summarized the life of natural man as "the war of each against all," with a resulting "continual fear of violent death, and the life of man solitary, poor, nasty, brutish and short." "I put for a general inclination of all mankind, a perpetual desire of power after power, that ceaseth only in death." "In the nature of man, we find three principal causes of quarrel. First, competition; second, diffidence; thirdly, glory. The first maketh men invade for gain; the second, for safety; the third, for reputation."

Cold war, hot war—that seems to be the sum total of world history in our time, perhaps of all history. No King of kings, no peace: "In those days there was no king in Israel; every man did what was right in his own eyes" (Judg. 21:25). Sovereign selves needed to be surrendered to the Sovereign Lord.

A fine, lyrical reference to Jacob's life is to be found in Hos. 12:2-6.

Little league baseball, supposed to be a recreational sport for boys, often turns into a grim struggle of parent against parent and parents against children which changes play into warfare.

Jas. 4:1-10 presents a surprising analysis of Jacob-mindedness. It begins, "What causes wars, and what causes fightings among you? Is it not your passions that are at war in your members? You desire and do not have; so you kill. And you covet and cannot obtain; so you fight and wage war." The whole passage is worth consulting.

Paul Tillich, the theologian, has taught us that sin is *estrangement,* a good label for Jacob's tangled relation to brother, to father-in-law and to Heavenly Father.

> Oh, what a tangled web we weave,
> When first we practice to deceive.

Two opposing philosophies of life: "To be is to hold my own against all comers," *versus* "to be is to belong to God."

Regarding Peniel, "the face of God," it is instructive to read what God said to Moses, "You cannot see me and live. . . . You shall see my back; but my face shall not be seen" (Exod. 33:20,

103

23). Meeting God face to face means death to natural man; in this meeting the man Jacob died and the new man, Israel, was born. Such an encounter calls for nothing less than a death and a resurrection. See Rom. 6:1-14.

In his book *The River Jordan,* archaeologist Nelson Glueck tells of sleeping overnight on Tell edh-Dhahab, which he identifies as Penuel, where the wrestling Jacob wrestled. "My Arab companions were very loath to have me sleep there alone, but would on no condition accompany me there to spend the night. They made their camp at the foot of the hill, warning me that if I persisted in my intention to sleep on top of it, a spirit (jinni) would seize me during the night, and that if indeed I did survive the ordeal I would wake up in the morning *majnun,* that is, possessed by the spirit. But here Jacob had wrestled during the night with his Adversary, being left alone only at the break of dawn" (pp. 112, 117).

### Striking Through to Outline

At some point in the brainstorming of the text, with allowance for the incubation which can take place in times of renunciation and interpolated activities, there should be a breakthrough into outline. For an outline on Jacob there are, of course, numerous possibilities. From among these I select three.

The first hinges upon the two most important places in the life of Jacob, Bethel, which means "the house of God," and Peniel, which means "the face of God":

I. Bethel: The house of God in the midst of our very human world of selfish striving and fearful flight
   A. The conflict, resulting in danger
   B. The flight
   C. The real but awkward presence of God

II. Peniel: The face of God breaking through the self-frustrations
   of our competitive striving
   A. Caught in the web of our own competitive cleverness
      1. Using up our hiding places
      2. At wit's end
   B. The meeting with God, the antagonist
   C. The capitulation: not killed, "let God rule," a new name
   D. The opening
      1. Reconciliation with our brother
      2. Life in history under the providence of God

A second approach to outline makes similar use of the two
names of the patriarch:

I. Jacob, "the supplanter," his own man
   A. Faces man in a competitive framework, in his own strength
      and cleverness
   B. Is confronted by a disturbing vision of God
      1. Does not fully understand it
      2. Makes a kind of treaty with God, resulting in an
         "armistice"
      3. The cold war continues
II. Israel, "let God rule," God's man
   A. Experiences the breakdown of his own resources
   B. Discovers human conflict to be the arena of God's judgment
   C. Survives the ultimate encounter
   D. Is reborn as selfish advantage drops away before service in
      God's design

A third outline emerges from the contrast between the two
opposing philosophies of life inherent in the narrative:

I. Life as a contest of wits and strength for selfish advantage
   A. Self as predator
   B. God as a convenient utility
   C. God as a disturbing Presence

II. Life as a network of human relationships
   A. Self as self-frustrating and self-destroying
   B. Others as enemies
   C. God as antagonist who breaks our self-will and blesses us
   D. Human reconciliation as goal and outcome

## Naming the Sermon

The title of the sermon on Jacob needs to have contemporary relevance: "Taking On All Comers"—"When God Overtakes Us"—"Fighting Against God"—"Overreaching Ourselves."

# 7

## Preaching on a Parable

Matthew summarizes a day of Jesus' teaching in these familiar words: "All this Jesus said to the crowds in parables; indeed he said nothing to them without a parable" (Matt. 13:34). Jesus spoke in parables, and the record of these story sermons holds fascination for us as well as for the crowds that first heard them. As a result we find ourselves turning to them with great frequency in our preaching.

But whereas Jesus spoke *in* parables, we speak *on* his parables. The difference may be enormous. What came in the beginning upon the people as a fresh burst of light may turn under our clumsy repetition into a gloomy drizzle of ancient maxims. To speak in parables required creativity of the highest order; yet to speak on them is not without its own creative requirements.

### Interpreting a Parable

As originally told to its first hearers, a biblical parable did not need to be explained. If successful, it struck home, producing contrition and change of life. If unsuccessful, it stiffened resistance and created or increased hostility. But it never left its hearers indifferent and unchanged.

*A case study.* Perhaps we can see the parables of Jesus more clearly if we look away from the New Testament entirely and study the best of the Old Testament parables—Nathan's story of the poor man's one little lamb in II Sam. 12:1-6. Here is a classical biblical parable unambiguously related to its original setting. It tells us much about the use and meaning of parables, wherever they may be found. See what it shows us:

The truth that Nathan was concerned to convey to David was personal truth that made a claim upon David. It demanded that David see himself with new insight as clearly as he would have seen another man in a like situation. It further demanded that David should act upon his new insight by repenting and changing his life. The truth that Nathan sought to convey was not a mere statement of objective fact. Neither was Nathan's truth a universal moral maxim or the reiteration of a timeless moral principle. It was dated and addressed. It was truth for David; it was truth for David at the exact point of time in which he had been guilty of the murder of Uriah to cover up his adultery with Uriah's wife. It was a highly particular, individual truth which came to David as a personal demand. *The truth of Nathan's parable was not the kind of truth that you merely believe; it was the kind of truth that you do—or shun at your peril.*

The truth that Nathan sought to convey to David was, moreover, unwelcome to David. He did not want to see it, and all other devices used by moralists and preachers would probably have failed to make him see it. Good advice and earnest exhortation would only have angered him. It is the nature of a guilty man that he rationalizes his guilt, that he makes himself an exception to universal moral maxims, and that he resists change and challenge by redoubling his defenses.

To penetrate David's emotional defenses, Nathan needed a special weapon that would take David off-guard and pierce his conscience before he could prepare himself. This Nathan created in the parable of the one little ewe lamb.

In creating this weapon he worked on two seemingly independent planes of moral truth: (1) David's memory of his sin with Bathsheba and against Uriah, and (2) the true-to-life story of a rich rancher who defrauded a poor peasant of his lamb. The first plane was the fact of David's recent action; as such it was lying like a sleeping serpent in the back of his guilty mind. The second plane was a story about another man, guilty of a monstrous crime of another sort, yet like David's crime in one respect: A great evil had been done by a man of wealth and power against a poor, common man who had no power.

Nathan told his story on the second plane, waiting for David's keen moral sense to condemn the wealthy sheep rancher for stealing and killing his peasant neighbor's lamb. To David the whole thing sounded like a case of foul injustice between two of his subjects, a case so flagrantly cruel as to call for his royal intervention and the inflicting of the death penalty. Precisely as David's anger reached its zenith, Nathan flicked the switch that caused the plane of his parable to intersect with the plane of David's guilty memory: "You are the man. [A man of royal wealth, with many wives.] You have smitten Uriah the Hittite with the sword, and have taken his wife to be your wife." The similarity was obvious; David could not evade it. Nathan's parable had effectively penetrated David's defenses.

Yet again, Nathan's parable was an act requiring moral courage of its spokesman. His audience—his sole audience—was a king with the power of life and death over his subjects. Nathan surely knew that his reward for his pains could be imprisonment or even execution. But he took his life in his hands, summoned his courage, and spoke the surgical truth with which God had entrusted him.

109

The truth of a parable, by enabling its hearers to see themselves in a new light, makes a personal claim upon them. The teller of the parable, in bringing his demanding truth home, requires moral courage and creative imagination of the highest order. He works at personal peril with a potentially or actually hostile audience who, in any case, are dead set against what he wants to tell them. His story must be skillfully contrived. It must be true to life. It must be analogous to the situation of his hearers, but at the same time different enough from the situation as they see it that they will not recognize themselves in the tale until the very end, when it is too late to save themselves from its point.

Nathan, his parable, and his audience of one come alive as a vivid event—but still in the past. The original power of the parable depended upon the element of surprise; David had not heard it before. It came fresh from the mind of Nathan and it was created specifically for his king. Preaching on Nathan's parable centuries later we run into certain difficulties. The story, fresh and original when David first heard it, is familiar to every Bible reader and church attender through frequent repetition. How can it still take a hearer by surprise, thus triggering in him an unwelcome and unexpected insight? The parable, once a weapon in the battle for a man's life, has become a museum piece, treasured for its literary beauty. To restore it to its original use in the lives of its present hearers will require a great deal more than simple retelling, as it will also require more than learned commentary.

If we have this difficulty with Nathan's parable, we have still other difficulties with the parables of Jesus in the Synoptic Gospels. Some Synoptic parables live on as literary units but without any record of the hearers or their life situation. It is as if Nathan's parable had lived, while David and his actions had suffered oblivion. How could we reconstruct Nathan's point in that case? Sometimes the evangelists, writing in the face of the church's needs, reset the parables of Jesus so as to address them to the evangelists' own contemporaries. How can we recover the original setting? If we cannot recover it, how can we be sure of Jesus' meaning?

It is these difficulties and others like them that have led to the abuse of allegorizing the parables. Irenaeus, for example, who lived in the second century, developed this elaborate exegesis of the laborers in the vineyard:

The first call to the workers represents the beginning of the created world, while the second symbolized the Old Covenant. The third call represents Christ's Ministry. The long lapse of time in which we now live is the fourth call, while the final call symbolizes the end of time. The vineyard is righteousness; the household, the Spirit of God; and the denarius, or "penny," is immortality.[1]

Allegorizing gives us "ornamental garments for religious commonplaces," said A. T. Cadoux; and this is a long way from the fresh, surprising insights of the original parables. While the parables of Jesus in the Synoptic Gospels may contain allegorical elements, they are not allegories; when interpreted as such, they are misconstrued.

The moralizing of the parables is an even more subtle danger. This was chiefly demonstrated by the nineteenth-century German scholar Adolph Jülicher, of whom A. M. Hunter writes:

Jülicher said that a parable exists to make one point. But what kind of point? His answer was: a general moral truth—the more general the better. The point of The Sons of the Bridechamber was:

[1] A. M. Hunter, *Interpreting the Parables* (Philadelphia: Westminster Press, 1960), p. 24.

111

"Religious sentiment is valuable only if it expresses the proper sentiment," Of the Unjust Steward: "Wise use of the present is the condition of a happy future." Yet the Man who went about Galilee drawing these innocuous morals was eventually spiked to a Cross. There is something far wrong here.[2]

Plainly, we are confronting a matter of technical biblical scholarship. The meaning of a parable is not to be picked up easily by a kind of homiletical hunch. The study of the latest scholarly commentaries becomes imperative.[3] We should make it a rule never to preach on a parable without consulting two or more good, up-to-date commentaries. If we could always be sure of the life situation to which the parable was originally addressed, we could also be sure of its meaning; but the recovery of that situation is a task so technical that it calls for the help of experts.

We do well also to realize that a parable has a recognizable literary structure. It is a popular story told to make a single point. As Professor Hunter has shown, the point applies to an area of truth to which the hearer is blind, employs an analogy in which the hearer sees, and, by hiding the unwelcome truth from the hearer until it is too late for him to guard against it, lures him to self-conviction.

In doing this the parables make frequent use of certain devices. There is a good deal of repetition which has the effect of building up the story toward a climax. There is

---

[2] *Ibid.*, pp. 38-39.
[3] The more helpful of these now seem to be: A. T. Cadoux, *The Parables of Jesus: Their Art and Use* (London: James Clark & Co., n.d.) ; Hunter, *Interpreting the Parables;* Joachim Jeremias, *The Parables of Jesus,* tr. by S. H. Hooke (New York: Charles Scribner's Sons, 1963) ; C. H. Dodd, *The Parables of the Kingdom* (London: Charles Scribner's Sons, 1935) .

contrast—as between the wise and foolish virgins, or the Phari-
see and the publican. There may be "the rule of three" (three
actors or groups of actors) which, together with "the rule of
end stress," throws the weight of the parable upon the third
servant in a parable like that of the talents. Do not ask, for
example, what it means to have five talents or two talents; the
"end stress" focuses alone upon the unprofitable servant with
one talent.

In the light of the forgoing discussion perhaps we can lay
down a few guiding principles:

(1) Study the parable to discover its single point. Guard
against allegorizing it and "making it walk on all fours."

(2) With the help of commentaries (especially needed with
parables) try to ascertain the situation in the life of Jesus to
which it was originally addressed; or, if that is inaccessible, the
situation in the life of the church to which it was readdressed
by the evangelist.

(3) In particular, study the resistance to truth—the spiritual
blindness of those to whom the parable was originally addressed
—and the manner in which the parable thrust like a rapier
through their defenses.

(4) Look for analogous situations in the life of your hearers
to which the point of the parable applies. For example, a
recent chapel sermon by a senior at Lexington Theological
Seminary used the parable of the ninety and nine sheep at the
close and as the climax of what at first appeared to be a topical
sermon on "Christians and Statistics." The preacher began by
reciting a page of apparently unrelated statistics—four out of
five marriages are happy, more than 60 percent of Americans
belong to a church, the average American income is above
$2,000 per year. Next, he asked what these statistics had in
common. Two things, he said. First, they seemed to bring

us comfort. Second, they ignored "the odd ball" who did not fit into the majority.

As a further step, the student preacher then recounted a painful incident in which he had not recognized the symptoms of distress in a recent conversation he had had in the home of a couple whose marriage blew apart shortly afterward; his mind had been so set on successful marriages that he had failed to see the breaking marriage right under his nose. He told this incident in realistic detail and with narrative skill. Finally, he concluded by reading the parable of the ninety and nine. This brought home the fact that Jesus was concerned not about the majority but about the "odd ball"—the unchurched American, the poor, the unhappy couple—and it resulted in the realization that the hearers (theological students and professors) were far more like the Pharisees than they wanted to admit.

(5) On occasions of unusual inspiration it may even be possible to invent a new parable—an analogous parable—which makes the point of the original but in a new setting and in a fresh way. While this new parable can never have the genius of the original, it may have new impact deriving from freshness and surprise, which were two marks of the original in its first telling.

### The Text

The parable of the talents is found in Matt. 25:14-30. We recognize how similar—and yet how different—it is to Luke 19:12-27, the parable of the pounds. In the Gospel of the Nazarenes we discovered an obvious recension of the talents: There were three servants, one who multiplied his master's money, a second who hid it, and a third who "squandered the money on harlots and flute-players; the first he commended,

114

the second he blamed, and the third is thrown into prison." [4]

## The Text in Context

Matthew gives us the five books of Christ to fulfill and super-sede the five books of Moses. Each book subdivides into narra-tive and discourse.[5] The parable of the talents takes its place within the discourse section of the fifth book. In the narrative portion of this fifth book of Christ, Jesus goes to Jerusalem and enters into the events of the final week. The mood is that of the hymn,

> Ride on! ride on in majesty!
> In lowly pomp ride on to die;
> O Christ, Thy triumphs now begin
> O'er captive death and conquered sin.

In the discourses of the fifth book, the theme is the end of the age and the last judgment. (The discourse section is Matt. 24:1–25:46; it is followed by the epilogue of Matthew's Gospel on the crucifixion and resurrection.) Detailed prophecies of the end of the age occupy Matt. 24:1-36. Exhortations to be prepared, as though living on the threshold of crisis, fill Matt. 24:37–25:30. The last judgment is depicted in Matt. 25:31-46. From such a setting one would suppose that the parable of the talents was a crisis parable, a teaching about living at the end of an epoch and on the threshold of God's new age. To quote Jeremias, "The catastrophe will come as unexpectedly as the nocturnal house-breaker, as the bridegroom arriving at midnight, the master of the house returning late from the

---

[4] Jeremias, *The Parables of Jesus*, p. 58.
[5] See my book *Preaching on the Books of the New Testament*, pp. 22-24.

wedding-feast, the nobleman returning from a far journey. See that you be not taken unawares!" [6]

So much for the literary context of the parable. Now turn to its context within the life of the church which made up the Gospel's earliest readers. What was their situation? They were living after the resurrection and ascension, in expectation of the Second Coming, many of them asking why Christ's return was so long delayed. This was perhaps the beginning of doubts which became exaggerated by the time of Second Peter—scoffers saying, "Where is the promise of his coming? For ever since the fathers fell asleep, all things have continued as they were from the beginning of creation" (II Pet. 3:4).

When we turn back to the parable in the light of its writer and first readers' living situation, we begin to see certain allegorical touches which reflect that situation: There are the Master's journey (Matt. 25:14), his return after a long delay and settling of accounts (vs. 19). The good and faithful servant enters into the joy of his Lord (vs. 23) —that is, he is justified and accepted. The worthless servant, in contrast, is to be cast into outer darkness where there will be weeping and gnashing of teeth (vs. 30); this is an obviously eschatological figure. These touches justify scholars in treating the parable of the talents as a parousia parable. Its message for the reader-audience of the late first century was a warning against slackness caused by the delay of Christ's return.

Turn in yet another direction. Who were the very first hearers of the parable as Jesus spoke it? They were obviously Jews; much had been entrusted to them, but in Jesus' day they were making little use of that trust. More specifically, the first hearers were probably moralistic Pharisees intent upon saving their own souls by scrupulous observance, but so selfish

---

[6] Jeremias, *The Parables of Jesus*, p. 63.

and exclusive that their religion was never really invested. Still more narrowly, Jeremias sees the parable as originally addressed to the scribes. He recalls Jesus' words to them in Luke 11:52, "Woe to you lawyers! for you have taken away the key of knowledge; you did not enter yourselves, and you hindered those who were entering."

Much had been entrusted to them: the Word of God; but like the servants in the parable, they would shortly have to render account of how they had used it in accordance with the will of God, or whether, like the third servant, they had frustrated the operation of the divine word by self-seeking and careless neglect of God's gift.[7]

Where Jesus was calling for a boulevard by which God's truth would go out and do commerce with the world, the scribes were busy setting up barriers to keep that truth from being contaminated by contact with the world.

## Spelling Out Some Textual Meanings

*Matt. 25:14.* "Called his servants and entrusted to them his property" (RSV). "Entrusted his property to their care" (Weymouth). "Handed his property over to them to manage" (Phillips). "Put his property in their hands" (Goodspeed). The servants thus became stewards in charge of a trust; they were managers of capital goods, responsible to their employer. Ostensibly this story is about money; but as a parable it merely uses money analogically to talk about another kind of trust. That trust is the entrusted word of God's truth. (The application was familiar to the early church, as is shown by I Tim. 6:20; II Tim. 1:12, 14; Titus 1:3; I Cor. 9:17; and Gal. 2:7).

[7] *Ibid.,* p. 62.

*Matt. 25:15.* "To one he gave five talents, to another two, to another one" (RSV). A talent was a measurement in weight; when applied to silver it had a certain value which is translated into its modern equivalent by Phillips and Goodspeed as a thousand dollars: "He gave one five thousand dollars, another two thousand and another one thousand" (Phillips). In the economy of Palestine in Jesus' day that was a vast sum, equal in our time to perhaps as many millions of dollars. (The pounds of Luke 19:12-27 are modest, being equal to no more than twenty dollars each.)

*Matt. 25:15.* "To each according to his ability" (RSV). This emphasis upon the differing abilities of the three servants seems marginal to the story, not central. Some preaching moves it to center and further confuses the original sense of the parable by translating "talents" from money into individual abilities. This is a distortion by which what is entrusted to each servant is his own abilities. In the original, the trust was the master's wealth, not any possession of the servants—not even their abilities; but the servants were to be held responsible for their trust, each according to his own differing abilities.

*Matt. 25:18.* "Dug in the ground and hid his master's money" (RSV). Money is not for hoarding. It is a medium of exchange to be used in buying and selling in the business world. The third servant was false to the nature of his trust—it was money, not a priceless art treasure to be kept intact just as it was; and he was also false to his abilities—he applied none of them.

*Matt. 25:19.* "Now after a long time" (RSV). Phillips sharpens the meaning by his paraphrase: "Some years later." This fits both the realism of the story and the eschatological hope of the early church which cherished the story.

118

*Matt. 25:16.* "Went at once and traded" (RSV). Goodspeed makes a more pointed translation: "Immediately went into business." This is obviously what the master had intended. He was not looking for men who would keep his money safe; he wanted it to be put to work earning more capital.

*Matt. 25:24-27.* "I knew you to be a hard man." This is the worthless servant's estimate of his master's character. As such it is woefully distorted by the servant's need to rationalize his own criminal neglect of his duty. He is to blame; he tries to shift the blame. Recognizing the mechanism of projection, we quickly suspect that the slothful servant himself was a hard man, trying by every hard-nosed device at his command to reap where he had not sown. The master, curiously, does not defend his character against this misrepresentation, but calmly points out that the servant's behavior was abysmally inconsistent with his professed conviction about his master.

*Matt. 25:29.* "For to every one who has will more be given." Most commentators treat this as an aside—a marginal remark which becomes diversionary when it is treated as the point of the parable. If, however, the entrusted money is an analogue for the Christian faith, the verse may be read as a central, though generalized, statement of its main point: He who invests his faith will grow in faith, while he who merely hoards and guards it will lose what little faith he has.

In this brief exegetical section of the present chapter, I have not discussed the eschatological passages since they had already come under review in our study of the context, in the previous section.

### Putting Yourself into the Text

Originally, it would appear, the parable was an open line through which God spoke to the Pharisees and their scribes. They were like the worthless steward who forsook his steward-

119

ship by hiding investment money in the ground. They could not see religion as creative risk-taking; they saw it as fortress-building.

In the early church, which was beginning to doubt the Second Coming, the parable spoke God's warning to those who neglected God's business and went on living as though Jesus might never return. The best one could do under that circumstance was to keep the trust intact in case it was ever required by its original owner. Meantime, the real concerns of life were elsewhere, with one's own affairs.

The *Gleichzeitigkeit* [8] of Christ can bring us into the dialogue at either level. We "good Christian people," especially we Christian leaders, are the self-styled "defenders of the faith." We are so often busy building fences for our creed when we ought to be laying highways for our God. Adventurous risk-taking in God's service requires creative churchmanship and prophetic conscience in carrying out his business in the secular world. We are the modern scribes and Pharisees.

Or, on the other hand, we may be latter-day Christians who live in a world from which Christ is absent. The world is not his; his "lordship" is a fiction—at least, as things now stand and in all probability will stand for a long time to come. His coming to us is postponed until after our physical death. Then it may happen, in which case we had better be ready to total up accounts. This we can do on a strictly legalistic basis by giving to God what belongs to him—without loss and without increment. If, as it turns out, God is not a ledger-keeper, but the spendthrift Father of Jesus Christ who poured out his life to the uttermost for the whole life of a man in the whole life of the world, our ledger-keeping attitude toward religion will have missed him altogether, both in this world and in the next.

[8] Contemporaneity or simultaneity.

## Finding the Parable's Internal Unity

*Aim:* To castigate a defensive, non–risk-taking attitude toward religious life; to encourage an adventurous investment of religion in the secular world.

*Proposition:* The man (or church) who will not risk the secular investment of his religion, though he expects God's approval, will come under God's judgment.

*Key verse:* "I was afraid, and I went and hid your talent in the ground."

## Uncovering the Parable's Dynamics

I. The trust
   A. The master's entrusting of his money to his servants
   B. God's entrusting of his word to Israel and the church
II. Contrasting attitudes toward the trust
   A. The faithfulness of the first two stewards
   B. The uselessness of the third. He took the trust seriously. He did not squander it selfishly. He guarded it and took no risks. He rationalized his motives and expected his master's approval. But he completely misunderstood his master's character and misconstrued the nature of what was entrusted to him—it was not to be kept safe but was to be put to work.
III. The master's judgment
   A. Acceptance of the faithful stewards' service
   B. Judgment upon the useless steward

## Brainstorming the Text

The defensive attitude of the third steward is seen in much misguided churchmanship: exclusiveness in church life at any of the following points—respectability, economic class, nationality, or race. The church existing for its own sake; advertising itself and seeking preferment in the community. Sunday

121

religion without weekday applications in vocation and citizenship. Selfish denominationalism in the face of Christian unity movements. The fear of submitting the Bible to scientific study; the call for blind faith.

In this, the church imitates the Old Testament Jews who built a hedge about the law, tithed mint, anise, and cummin to win merit in the sight of God, and followed out a policy of selfish exclusiveness. Says the Jewish commentator Rabbi Klausner, "The Judaism of that time had no other aim than to save the tiny nation, the guardian of great ideals, from sinking into the broad sea of heathen culture." This was the program of scrupulous Pharisaism.

Just to suppose: What if the third steward had invested his money and lost it? Would his master then have praised or condemned him? Jesus did not press the analogy that far for the simple reason that it did not apply in the area of truth to which it referred. Since the trust was the entrusted Word of God, Jesus, no doubt, believed with Isaiah:

> For as the rain and the snow come down from heaven,
>   and return not thither but water the earth,
> making it bring forth and sprout,
>   giving seed to the sower and bread to the eater,
> so shall my word be that goes forth from my mouth;
>   it shall not return to me empty,
> but it shall accomplish that which I purpose,
>   and prosper in the thing for which I sent it. (Isa. 55:10-11.)

The success of the investment depends not upon the wisdom of the investor but on the investment's getting a chance to work by being invested. It does not need protection—it needs opportunity.

A church defending the faith from error is not unlike physicians huddled together in a hospital with the sick world outside, refusing to risk infection. We see the attitude in some teachers who are bent upon preserving the English language from damage rather than turning it into dynamite for blasting out old wrongs; and in librarians who are frustrated museum curators, really resenting the circulation and reading of their precious volumes. In our democracy it is easy to fall into the same error; we do this when we guard its institutions rather than employ its processes. This, in fact, is like building fences against weeds, when what is needed is to cultivate the garden.

Just as there is mother love and smother love between parent and child, so there is a kind of loyalty to God's word which smothers it.

Arnold Toynbee, renowned historian, not long ago said that America had changed from being a frontier to being a fortress. The words on the base of the "New Colossus" represent the earlier, risk-taking attitude. How many Americans today are eager to invite the world's displaced persons as these words do?

> Give me your tired, your poor,
> Your huddled masses, yearning to breathe free.

It is more tempting to defend a position than to share it, but it is also more perilous in the long run. Alcoholics Anonymous says that a man can keep his sobriety only by sharing it. How about Christian faith? Unless we invest it in the secular world, we may lose what little faith we have.

### Striking Through to Outline

*A deductive approach to outline (an example):*

I. Interpret the parable and make the point in relation to pharisaic exclusiveness

II. Show the relation of his point to us by "reaudiencing" the parable
   A. A church composed largely of landlords has recently turned a cold shoulder to visiting tenants because "they are not our kind of people." Christ came to save sinners, not to comfort the respectable. But what of the risk, if they were accepted?
   B. "Keep the church out of politics and economics. Just preach the gospel," is a criticism often leveled by well-meaning laymen against certain brands of prophetic preaching. To invest the gospel in vocation and citizenship is to risk controversy; let's keep it peaceful here!
   C. "These unity movements in the church are probably a good thing, but I hope our church stays out. We might lose our distinctive witness if we went in."

*An inductive approach to outline (an example):*

I. Begin with a contemporary situation of sedate church life resisting the costly community investment that Christ calls for. For example, a downtown church is about to pull out of its property in a declining urban area and move to a prosperous suburb, leaving the urban area unchurched. The situation needs to be depicted in some detail, so that the emotional resistance of the hearers gets a chance to rise, and so that the urge toward self-preservation will become paramount.
II. Simply retell the parable of the talents (making sure to use *dollars* and *investments* instead of *talents* and *trust*). If well told, the parable will make its own point. No need to belabor the moral.

*A more conventional outline (an example):*

I. What the third steward did
   A. In contrast to the two
   B. In contrast with a wastrel

II. Why he did it
   A. His responsibility impressed him more with the fear of what he might lose than with the opportunity of what he might gain
   B. He mistook the nature of the treasure he guarded; it was for investment, not for hoarding
III. How he misjudged
   A. In attempting to justify his fears he was uncharitable and mistaken in judging his master
   B. A man who thought himself safe was condemned

In the above outline the power of the sermon will depend upon weaving the life situation of the hearers into the warp of the parable at every strand. The suspense of the denouement must be kept for the end.

### Naming the Sermon

Here are a few of many possible titles: "Christ and Creative Insecurity," "From Frontier to Fortress," "Religion Follows the Frontier," "Salting Away Your Faith."

# 8

## Preaching on a Miracle

To the ancient Hebrews and early Christians, it would appear, a miracle was an aid to faith. To our science-oriented contemporaries it is an obstacle. Whereas the ancients looked for miracles and reveled in them, we are apt to look upon an alleged miracle with suspicion. The difference lies in our presuppositions about the laws of nature. For the ancients there were no inviolable laws of nature to be ruptured. For us there are such unbreakable laws. William Temple, the late Archbishop of Canterbury, stated the modern problem succinctly:

> The naïve religious view is that God made the world and imposed laws upon it, which it invariably observes unless He intervenes to modify the operation of His own laws. From this naïve point of view springs the suggestion that it would better comport with the infinite Majesty of God that He should from the outset impose such laws as would never stand in need of modification.[1]

From such a view—with or without God in the picture—it is but a short step to the modern dogma of millions: *Miracles do not happen*. When, therefore, a man stands up to preach to

[1] William Temple, *Nature, Man and God* (London: MacMillan, 1951), p. 267.

such people from a biblical miracle, he is confronted by a mind-set in his hearers which turns back his words like steel armor-plate blunting and shedding the arrows of an attacking medieval force. In the face of this mind-set many modern ministers have given up preaching on the miracles. They acknowledge the depth of the problem by avoiding it.

To be sure, there are thousands, perhaps millions, of church-goers who resist the modern dogma, or at least modify it to read: Miracles do not happen now; but in Bible times they did happen. To this they may unconsciously add the implication: If you do not believe in miracles, your faith is suspect. This fundamentalistic mind-set, while thought by its adherents to be "true to the Bible," is at least as far from the biblical point of view as its secular counterpart. For in this light miracles do not so much *aid* faith as *test* it. It would not be improper to call this an inquisitional view of miracles, more concerned with ferreting out heretics than with spreading or deepening the faith. Before this mind-set, as before the secular counterpart, ministers tend to shrink back into silence. Hence, on a second account, miracles are avoided in the pulpit.

### Interpreting a Miracle

What is the biblical point of view? To begin with, there is no one word for miracle in the Bible; and there is none carrying the implication of a divine lawbreaker. The Bible knows nothing of two ultimates: Law and God. It knows only one ultimate: God, acting in the world and in history according to his sovereign will. Hebrew words sometimes translated as "miracle" are more accurately rendered "sign" (את, *eth*) [2] and "wonder" (מופת, *mopheth*) [3] or (פלא, *pala*) .[4] In the Septuagint

[2] Exod. 4:8.
[3] Exod. 7:9.
[4] Exod. 3:20.

127

Old Testament these were translated as σημεῖον (sēmeion) and τέρας (teras), also meaning "sign" and "wonder." The Greek New Testament takes over these two words from the Septuagint,[5] then adds two others: δύναμις (dynamis),[6] "mighty work," and ἔργον (ergon),[7] "work." To summarize in English translation, the Bible speaks of "signs and wonders" and of "works" and "mighty works."

The Pharisees on several occasions asked Jesus to perform a miracle; that was the meaning of their request for a sign.[8] Evidently, from their point of view, Jesus had hitherto done nothing miraculous in their eyes. Jesus himself told them, as we have just seen, that no sign would be given them. The reason for this, in the simplest terms, is that an event, even though it might be out of the ordinary, *had to be seen with the eyes of faith* in order to be a sign of God's presence to the beholder. "It should be said again and again: a divine action of quite ordinary appearance, visible only to the believer, is a miracle. On the contrary, a phenomenon which is extraordinary, amazing, inexplicable, but unrelated to faith, is not one." [9]

A miracle has to be seen by eyes of faith; to the unbelieving the event is no miracle. Take for example the greatest miracle of the New Testament, the resurrection of Christ. It has often been noted that the risen Christ appeared only to those who had loved him. Why not to his enemies one may ask. A. Leonard Griffith puts the matter in dramatic form:

Imagine the consternation of Caiaphas and Pilate and the Centurion confronted by this man whom they had crucified three days

[5] Acts 2:22; Luke 23:8.
[6] Mark 9:39.
[7] Matt. 11:2. Translated "deeds" in RSV.
[8] Matt. 16:1-4; 12:38-39; Mark 8:11-12; Luke 11:16.
[9] M. Carrez in *A Companion to the Bible*, ed. by J. J. von Allmen (New York: Oxford University Press, 1958), p. 270.

earlier. Would they not have sunk to their knees in terror, blubber-
ing out their repentance and crying aloud for mercy? No, they
would not. They would have dismissed the thing as a hallucination
or else roared in anger over the failure of the executioners to do
their job properly. How, indeed, could they have recognized the
risen Christ when many of his own followers failed to recognize
him? In literal truth they did not have the spiritual vision to discern
the living presence of Jesus. They bear out the Master's own words,
"If they do not hear Moses and the prophets, neither will they be
convinced if someone should rise from the dead." [10]

In confirmation of the insight that miracles are for eyes
of faith, it will be seen that miracles are not uniformly distributed over the whole range of biblical history, but that they
cluster about pivotal events and persons in the drama. There
are four such clusterings: (1) The exodus and the entrance
into Canaan, (2) the prophetic reforms of Elijah and Elisha,
(3) the exile, and (4) the introduction of the New Israel under
Jesus and the apostles. All four periods of biblical history provided deep and unforgettable experiences of God for those
who responded in faith. Indeed, there is a still more fundamental clustering of all Old Testament events about the exodus
and of New Testament events about the resurrection. These
were the two great miracles of the Bible. Everything else participates in these and derives its fundamental meaning from
them.

Biblical miracles clustering about pivotal events and towering
personalities in the biblical drama are recognized only by eyes
of faith. From this it follows that the interpretation of a miracle
does not lie in answering the question, How do you explain

[10] Griffith, *Barriers to Christian Belief* (New York: Harper & Row, 1962),
pp. 82-83.

it? The hope back of that question is the hope of remaining outside the miracle, objective and judging, uninvolved. The uninvolved are also the uncomprehending. If we persist in asking the wrong question of the miracles in the Bible, we will go on getting the wrong answers. There is a better question: What does it mean? Better still, What does it mean for me? There is the involvement of faith, in which alone is understanding in the realm of personal truth—that is, revelatory or redemptive truth.

The clue to the meaning of a miracle is fortunately provided in the Gospels themselves. The cursing of the barren fig tree, an incident in Jesus' ministry, is reported by the evangelists on the one hand as a miracle and on the other hand as a parable. (The miracle in Mark 11:12-14, 20-25 and Matt. 21:18-19 becomes the parable of Luke 13:6-9.) This is just the clue we need, for it leads to the insight that the rules for interpreting a miracle are basically the same as those for interpreting a parable. A miracle, one might say, is an acted parable done to make one point. That point was registered in a context; therefore we have to pay close attention to the audiencing or re-audiencing of the miracle, as we do of the parable. And, as with the parable, we had best do our work of interpreting only after the most painstaking consultation of scholars who have devoted special attention to the miracles.[11]

The point of a miracle, as of a parable, is active, divine truth making its claim felt in a human life. Harry Emerson Fosdick,

[11] Among these you will want to consider Reginald H. Fuller, *Interpreting the Miracles* (Philadelphia: Westminster Press, 1963); Robert M. Grant, *Miracle and Natural Law in Graeco-Roman and Early Christian Thought* (Amsterdam: North Holland Publishing Co., 1952); Alan Richardson, *The Miracle-Stories of the Gospels* (New York: Harper & Row, 1942); S. V. McCasland, *By the Finger of God* (New York: Macmillan, 1951); C. S. Lewis, *Miracles* (New York: Macmillan, 1947).

in his memorable lecture at Yale on "Miracle and Law," struck the ringing note:

Jesus never called on his followers as a test of discipleship to believe in narratives of other people's marvelous deeds, but he did insistently call on them to manifest in their own lives superhuman power, so that they might not have to scale down their expectations and achievements to the level of ordinary life. He did not expect them so much to believe in miracles as to work them. . . .

What, then, was the abiding conviction which our forefathers at their best were expressing when they thought and talked in terms of miracles? They were believing in the providence of God and in his immediate presence and activity in his world. They were saying that life so divinely ordered never can be ironed flat, reduced to the rigid limitations of the ordinary, but that always expectations must include events of "luminous surprise." [12]

## The Text

The miracle to be studied in this chapter is the feeding of the five thousand. The importance of this miracle to the early church is amply attested by its appearance in all four Gospels: Mark 6:30-44; Matt. 14:13a-21a; Luke 9:10-17; and John 6:1-13. Add to that emphasis the miracle of the feeding of the four thousand which appears in two of the Gospels (Mark 8:1-10 and Matt. 15:32-39) and one discovers a singular stress upon the feeding of multitudes in the gospel records. The literary device of "the doublet," sometimes resorted to by scholars in an effort to explain the feeding of the five thousand plus the feeding of the four thousand in the same two Gospels, leaves the fundamental question unanswered—why Mark and Mat-

[12] Harry Emerson Fosdick, *The Modern Use of the Bible* (New York: Macmillan, 1924), pp. 156-57.

thew should have used such similar narratives in their two short books, only a few verses apart.

## The Text in Context

The events of Jesus' life, as seen in the Synoptics, were moving rapidly toward the climax and close of his ministry to Galilee. Herod had begun asking about him, and not merely out of idle curiosity. He had slain John the Baptist with his beheading knife. And now another—or could it be the same? —prophet was marching over Galilee electrifying great crowds. To Herod's fevered, superstitious brain, this was a matter to be looked into. Opposition from the Jewish authorities had grown to its own fever pitch. Jesus needed to take his disciples aside for a quiet day in the country to compose and prepare them for the building crisis. And since the disciples had just returned from their own tour of Galilee, he needed time and quiet to hear their reports. But the eager multitudes overran their retreat. With these masses Jesus was never more popular, or more misunderstood.

As Matthew and Mark record the events, Jesus and his little band turned immediately from the feeding of the five thousand to the Gentiles of the Decapolis. In sailing over the lake the disciples ran into a violent storm, then saw Jesus coming to them, treading safely over the turbulent waters and rescuing Peter from its angry depths. Both Mark and Matthew make it quite clear by their setting that the feeding of the four thousand, which followed shortly, was in Gentile territory and as such was a part of Jesus' mission to Gentiles. Thereafter events move rapidly to Peter's confession at Caesarea Philippi, then to the transfiguration and thence to the closing out of the northern mission and the beginning of the last journey to Jerusalem.

The sense of impending end is no less vivid in Luke's account. He makes the feeding of the five thousand do service for both miracles, though placing it in a Gentile setting. Then he quickly sketches in the concluding events of the northern ministry and Jesus' prediction of martyrdom.

In the Fourth Gospel, the setting of the miracle is less a matter of events than of theme. The feeding of the multitude is placed over against the Passover of the Jews (John 6:4); at the same time it is interpreted against the ancient gift of manna in the wilderness and in terms of a long discourse on Jesus as the bread of life. The sense of conflict with the Jewish authorities is strong here, as in all of John's Gospel. But Jesus' popularity with the masses is just as menacing because it is so misguided—as is shown in the incident in which they tried to force a crown upon him. Dovetailed into this long chapter on the bread of life in John, the account of the storm at sea occurs, symbolically representing the mounting crisis in which Jesus and his little band were being engulfed.

Two things appear in all accounts: the meager resources of the disciples—their little faith, for all that was demanded of them; and the majesty of Christ, who takes their little and multiplies it to equal and more than equal the people's need, and who mysteriously rides upon the storm.

## Spelling Out Some Textual Meanings

Mark 6:30-44 will be followed as the central text, with comments on the versions in the other three Gospels as they may be called for.

*To get away from the crowds* (Mark 6:30-32). Although Herod had beheaded John and was looking for Jesus, the immediate reason for the retreat which Jesus proposed was that he and the twelve might make a quiet time in which to review the twelve's recent two-by-two itinerary of Galilee (vss. 7-13).

133

Things were so hectic in Capernaum that "they had no leisure even to eat," let alone talk in a meeting of their own. This motive for the meeting is recorded by Mark alone. Matthew implies that John's execution furnished the motive (Matt. 14:12-13).

*The crowds foil their attempt* (Mark 6:33). Jesus and his party would have had no success walking to their retreat; a boat offered the only possible escape, but even that failed. The people running around the shore arrived ahead of them.

*A day's mass meeting followed* (Mark 6:34-36). Jesus' compassion overcame the plans for the day, and out of his compassion for the people, he devoted the time to teaching them. The disciples were deprived of their private meeting. There was perhaps some eagerness to get rid of the crowd behind their suggestion that Jesus send the throng home as suppertime approached.

*Jesus' request to feed the crowds seems absurd to the disciples* (Mark 6:37-38). How could they feed this huge crowd of five thousand? (Matthew indicated that there were five thousand *men,* plus an uncounted number of women and children [Matt. 14:21].) It was obvious to them that there were no food resources at hand adequate to supply such a throng. The only other alternative was to buy food; but to feed them would cost forty dollars (which we need to multiply greatly to get a modern equivalent—William Barclay has estimated that it was a workingman's wages for half a year). Who had that kind of money in this impromptu situation? Jesus, it seems, had not expected them to buy food, but simply to use the resources at hand. John alone reports that a mere boy who happened to be in the crowd had five flat round loaves made from barley flour and two smoked fish (John 6:9). That was the extent of their supply for the impossible demand.

134

*Jesus multiplies these few loaves and fish until they feed the multitude* (Mark 6:41-42). In all the accounts Jesus prayed, broke the bread, and distributed it. This is the action of the Lord's Supper as well—blessed and brake and gave. Mark and Matthew used "blessed" (the Greek word forms the basis of our word for "eulogy"). The customary Jewish prayer at mealtime was, "Blessed art thou, O Lord our God, king of the world, who has brought forth bread from the earth." The Jew, it will be noticed, blessed God, not the bread, which presumably is already blessed since God gave it. John 6:11 and Mark 8:6 report that Jesus "gave thanks"; the Greek word used in both passages is the basis for our English word "Eucharist." The eucharistic meaning of the passage is made quite explicit in John, but it seems clearly implied in the Synoptics as well. Jesus took their little and made it adequate to the people's need.

*An abundance remains* (Mark 6:43-44.) Leftovers filled twelve baskets. The baskets indicated are *kofinoi* (κόφινοι), the equivalent of knapsacks. According to Barclay, Jews always carried them when traveling. The twelve baskets that were filled evidently were the disciples' own knapsacks. In giving, they had received more bountifully than they had given!

This is a simple story. The allegorical touches and historical allusions, particularly in its Johannine form, make it clear that there are several levels of meaning to be read within the story. There is first the experience of God's bounty which little men with small resources often discover when they give what they have and find it miraculously multiplied. Elisha once fed a hundred men in like fashion (II Kings 4:42-44). Perhaps this incident from the Old Testament was fresh in the minds of Jesus and the disciples.

A second level of meaning is eucharistic. In John, it makes

Jesus the new Passover sacrifice and the new manna from heaven. But in all the Gospels, the symbolic action of the Lord's Supper is present. Besides, the loaves and fish came very early in the life of the church to have eucharistic meanings. This can be seen from inscriptions in the Roman catacombs, and from ancient floor mosaics at et-Tabgha near the traditional site of the miracle.

A third level of meaning is eschatological. We noticed the sense of impending end that environs the incident in the Synoptic Gospels. Beyond this, however, a favorite Jewish symbol of the kingdom of God was the messianic banquet. Jesus himself used it, as reported in Matt. 22:1-14 and Luke 14:16-24.

## Putting Yourself into the Text

In reading this miracle we are to identify ourselves neither with Jesus nor with the eager multitudes, but with the disciples who, while wanting Jesus to themselves, had little faith that the needs of the people before them could be met, either by their own resources or by his. Whether we stay to see the miracle depends upon the degree to which we really bring forth what resources we do have and commit them to the One who can multiply them. Many who have done just this testify to the fact that such miracles do happen, and that they keep on happening. As churchmen, many modern disciples seriously doubt if the church is relevant to the people in the twentieth century and are frantically but unbelievingly looking for some way of making it relevant. If we are like these, we are saying, "But what are these among so many?" Is it inconceivable that Christ himself, the bread of life, may be enough; that he may be able "far above all that we ask or think" to meet man's need—if only we will let him speak?

## Finding the Internal Unity of the Text

*Aims:* (1) To demonstrate the divine multiplication of our meager resources when we engage them in the work of Christ and depend upon his power.

(2) To present the Communion as a sacrament in which the presence and power of the living Christ may be experienced as filling up all our lack.

(3) To see the goal of history in Christ and his provision in infinite compassion for the needs of all who come to him, even though we are his reluctant and ill-equipped helpers.

*Propositions:* (1) Our Christian commission is measured not by our meager resources but by the dimensions of the world's needs and by the power of Christ.

(2) The Communion meals reenact the empowering presence of Christ by which our human little is gathered into God's bounty and made abundantly adequate for the service of people and for our own sustenance.

(3) In the midst of human want and political pressures on a seemingly overwhelming scale, Christ spreads his holy supper as a foretaste and promise of the messianic banquet: i.e., Christ himself is, in the words of Teilhard de Chardin, the "Omega Point" toward which history is moving.

The above objectives and themes are stated in such a way as to reflect the three levels of meaning which may be read in the miracle. The aim and proposition for any one sermon, obviously, should be taken from the same level of meaning: i.e., Aim Number One should match Proposition Number One.

## Uncovering the Dynamics of the Text

As reported by the Synoptic Gospels and enlarged by the Fourth Gospel, there are a number of tensions in the miracle of the feeding of the five thousand: (1) The peril of Jesus under Herod Antipas, who had just slain John the Baptist and who was now looking for Jesus. (2) Jesus' popularity with the crowd, based unfortunately upon their misconception of his mission and teaching, and eventuating in their effort to make him their king. (3) The unpreparedness and inadequacy of the disciples in the face of the people's need; their desire, in consequence, to dismiss the crowd.

The movement of the passage begins with the attempt of Jesus and his disciples to retreat to a quiet place for a conference among themselves. (The twelve had just returned from their two-by-two tour of Galilean towns; they were anxious to talk with their Master and he was anxious to hear their reports.) The insistent multitudes, however, poured out of the villages and inundated the retreat; Jesus, sensing their leaderless condition, spent the day in teaching and healing. Then came eventide, fatigue, and hunger. Jesus had been "feeding" the people all day long; he now commanded his disciples to feed their physical hunger. The disciples shrank back before such a demand; their resources were pitifully meager. Nonetheless Jesus took what they had, blessed and brake and gave, and all the multitudes were fed with enough left over to supply the knapsacks of the disciples for another day.

## Brainstorming the Text

*The first approach.* AIM No. 1: To demonstrate the multiplication of our meager resources, when we engage them in the work of Christ and depend upon his power. PROPOSITION No. 1: Our Christian commission is measured not by our meager resources but by the dimensions of the world's needs and by the power of Christ.

The perfect text, from Paul, for this sermon is Phil. 4:13, "I can do all things in him who strengthens me." Here was a man who matched himself single-handed against the hostility of the

138

Judaizers and the paganism of the Roman Empire to turn the Mediterranean Sea into a Christian lake. The staggering audacity of what he undertook and what he envisioned and accomplished is another instance of the multiplication of a man's little when it is engaged in the work of Christ. Many of the former realms of Christendom—Turkey and the Near East—are now lost to the church. What Paul won in a single lifetime alone almost staggers our faith when we contemplate reconquering it. How many mission boards, how many missionaries, how many dollars will we have to hold before we even think of making a beginning with that missionary task?

Lewis Smythe, who spent twenty-five years in China, tells a dramatic story coming out of World War II. There was need for a million blankets in Free China and no way of providing them. A producers' cooperative movement tackled the task. An old-fashioned spinning wheel, such as our American grandmothers used 150 years ago, was located. A Chinese engineer trained in Scotland streamlined it and mass produced the functional copy until he had five thousand spinning wheels—which nobody in China knew how to operate. An assistant set up instruction classes in which fifteen hundred women were taught the art of spinning with these wheels, and were sent out to instruct others. In homes all over Free China wheels were soon spinning and crude looms were weaving narrow strips which were then sewn together to make whole blankets—until there were one million of these blankets each year for six years and war's end.

There are vast works of Christian faith needing to be done: slum clearance, urban renewal, political reform of city governments, public health and sanitation, city beautification. Instead of focusing upon our meager resources, perhaps we could focus upon the imperatives of the task and tackle them with the energy

139

born of faith. There is little in any of these realms, it would seem, that could not be accomplished as if by miracle—"this is the victory that overcomes the world, our faith" (I John 5:4).

The work of a bantamweight Indian weighing barely ninety pounds (Mahatma Gandhi) was to oppose the awesome and formidable authority of the British Empire and wrestle from it the independence of his country. What meager resources; what a miraculous outcome—a resolution accomplished without force of arms, brought about instead by "soul force."

The missionaries of the church and the Peace Corps workers now out among the nations are daily reliving the miracle of the feeding of the five thousand. The recent feat of missionary Dr. Victor Rambo in performing ten thousand eye operations per year, year after year, restoring sight to cataract-blinded eyes, is only one astounding instance of it.

*The second approach.* AIM No. 2: To present the Communion as a sacrament in which the presence and power of the living Christ may be experienced as filling up our lack. PROPOSITION No. 2: The Communion meal reenacts the empowering presence of Christ by which our human little is gathered into God's bounty and made abundantly adequate for the service of people and for the sustaining of the servants themselves.

"Who is sufficient for these things?" (II Cor. 2:16), Paul asked as he confronted his Christian commission in a pagan culture. How often we echo his question, turning it into a cry of despair: "What is that among so many?" It is the same question as the one put by the disciples to Jesus in our text. And yet it is precisely this mood of emptiness and need that is one of the best preparations for the empowering presence of Christ in the Lord's Supper. If we come to his table in our emptiness and need, he may be able to fill us; whereas if we come in pride at our accomplishments and merits, he can do nothing because we need nothing.

Parents face their teen-age children these days—perhaps they have always done so in some measure—feeling totally bankrupt: "I don't understand them! I don't know what to do with or for them!" That is a good sense of emptiness to bring to the communion table.

Recently a young minister told of a painful visit which he had just made to the bedside of a man known to be dying of cancer. The patient also knew that he was dying. And yet, said the young minister, he himself tried every device he could think of to avoid the topic uppermost in both their minds, fumbling for one trivial topic of conversation after the other. Finally, when he had exhausted all the topics he could think of, his eye caught sight of a shotgun hanging on the bedroom wall. "I suppose you are fond of hunting?" he lamely commented. "Yes," came the reply from the bed, "but I don't suppose I will ever go hunting again." The unwanted question was squarely in the young minister's lap; he could avoid it no longer. If he met that dying man's need in any degree, it was not from his own meager resources.

The suggestion is simply this: Come to the Communion meal hungry and needy. This can be done by a simple rehearsal of the stinging inadequacy which we are currently feeling in some real-life struggle we are having as we seek to do our Christian duty in a complex and difficult time.

*The third approach.* AIM NO. 3: To celebrate the Communion meal as an eschatological sacrament; in other words, to celebrate this meal as the foreshadowing of the messianic banquet—that is, to see the goal of history in Christ's compassion. PROPOSITION No. 3: Christ himself is the "Omega Point" toward which all

141

history moves; it is he and not we who will bring in the kingdom.

It is not hard for us to translate into our own time the meanings of the miracle in its original setting: Herod Antipas, with blood on his hands, seeking Jesus; the leaderless masses, ignorant, hungering, and needy. This in our times is the looming threat of the totalitarian state and its massive military Moloch shaking its nuclear fist—the whole sociopolitical problem of our troubled world. More, it is the problem of exploding populations, of decaying cities, of juvenile delinquency, and other manifestations from masses of people for whom life threatens to shatter into meaningless fragments. It is so easy for our contemporary sense of history to get lost in futility and despair.

Perhaps we need nothing so much as a sense of meaning in our contemporary history. This, for Christian faith, is supplied by Christ, whose compassion is the goal of history. Between that compassion with its humanization and warming of relationships on the one side, and the cold mechanization of life on the other side, an Armageddon is raging. Notice this tendency toward mechanization as described by Teilhard de Chardin:

> We have "mass movements"—no longer the hordes streaming down from the forests of the north or the steppes of Asia, but "the Million" scientifically assembled. The Million in rank and file on the parade ground; the Million standardized in the factory; the Million motorized—and all this only ending up with Communism and National-Socialism and the most ghastly fetters. So we get the crystal instead of the cell; the ant-hill instead of brotherhood.[13]

Just as Christ entered human history centuries ago to do battle against these devilish forces and to draw all men unto himself as the true, liberating goal of history, so he now con-

[13] Pierre Teilhard de Chardin, *The Phenomenon of Man*, tr. by Bernard Wall, (New York: Harper & Row, 1959), pp. 256-57.

142

tinues to do battle against this organized death and to lead men
toward their real life. To continue from Teilhard de Chardin:

> Enormous powers will be liberated in mankind by the inner
> play of its cohesion: though it may be that this energy will still be
> employed discordantly tomorrow, as today and in the past. Are
> we to foresee a mechanizing synergy under brute force, or a
> synergy of sympathy? Are we to foresee man seeking to fulfill
> himself collectively upon himself, or personally on a greater than
> himself? Refusal or acceptance of Omega? [14]

The Scriptures present Christ both as Alpha—creative source
—and Omega—end and goal. This is a bold faith, needing bold
proclamation. It does not relieve life of tension or danger, but
it shows men where the battle is, girds them for it, and gives
them heart to engage the enemy.

Winfred Ernest Garrison in his ninety-first year published a
volume of poetry opening with a poem which sounds this same
note:

> Thy sea, O God, so great,
> My boat so small.
> It cannot be that any happy fate
> Will me befall
> Save as Thy goodness opens paths for me
> Through the consuming vastness of the sea.
>
> Thy winds, O God, so strong,
> So slight my sail.
> How could I curb and bit them on the long
> And salty trail
> Unless Thy love were mightier than the wrath
> Of all the tempests that beset my path?

[14] *Ibid.*, p. 288.

Thy world, O God, so fierce,
    And I so frail.
Yet, though its arrows threaten oft to pierce
    My fragile mail,
Cities of refuge rise where dangers cease,
Sweet silences abound, and all is peace.[15]


## Striking Through to Outline

The movement of the passage supplies the easiest and most natural path to the outline of the sermon, which goes through four phases:

I. The need: the structures of power and the hunger of the people
II. Our meager resources and our still more meager faith
III. Jesus Christ himself the source and supply
IV. Our surprising discovery: the need is met, we ourselves are fed


The success of the sermon will depend upon the realism and detail with which the basic situation of the Scriptures is made contemporaneous to us. The section on "Brainstorming the Text" has attempted to illustrate this, at least in part.

One approach to this sermon may follow the pattern of a diamond with many facets. First the diamond as a whole is presented in the fundamental pattern of the miracle. After which the jewel turns first one facet and then another to our contemplation as this truth is shown at work on the three levels just discussed.

Three separate sermons may be derived from the miracle. This pinpointed approach, by attempting less, may actually accomplish more. The success of the sermon depends funda-

[15] Winfred Ernest Garrison, *Thy Sea So Great* (St. Louis: Bethany Press, 1965), p. 13.

mentally upon the sharpness of the aim and the concreteness of the basic contemporary situation to which it is addressed. The standpoint of the minister and of his people is that of the disciples, confronting their situation with meager resources.

## Naming the Sermon

"Bread of the World," "Feeding Multitudes," "Structures of Power and the Hunger of Peoples," and "History with and Without a Point" are all possible titles.

# 9

## Preaching on a Short Text

Every scripture which serves as the basis of a sermon is a text. It may be long or short. The distinction between textual and expository preaching, based on length alone, is artificial and should be abandoned. All biblical preaching is at one and the same time textual and expository; it is based upon a text which it expounds.

The short text has had a place in Christian preaching from earliest times, but its use to the exclusion of longer passages is a homiletical heresy of recent development. The heresy was greatly aided by the division of the Bible into numbered chapters and verses. Division into chapters did not take place until the thirteenth century; it was the work of Stephen Langston, Archbishop of Canterbury. Further division into verses waited another three hundred years. A French printer, Robert Étienne, in 1550 divided his fourth edition of the Greek New Testament into 7,959 verses set up as paragraphs. William Whittingham did the same for his revision of the New Testament in 1557, and the Geneva Bible which came out in 1560 extended verse numberings to the Old Testament and Apocrypha as well. Such verse numbering is a convenient tool for ready reference, but it is obviously no criterion for the measurement of a text proper to a sermon.

Prior to this division of the Bible into chapters and verses, the units of scripture which would have commended themselves to Christian preachers would have been the *pericopes,* longer passages chosen primarily for liturgical purposes. The Jews did this for the Old Testament long before the Christian community had written its scripture or started to use the New Testament in a liturgical manner. By the time of Jesus this had been done for the Torah, and the process was well under way by which it was being done for the Prophets.

The development of the Christian year and the assigning of particular passages of scripture to be read Sunday by Sunday the year around followed in due course. The units of scripture thus assigned for liturgical purposes naturally became the units to be expounded in sermons. These units were large blocks of scripture.

After chapter and verse numberings were introduced, it was not long until it became the fashion to preach upon shorter and shorter texts. Broaddus reports that a seventeenth-century Englishman, John Howe, preached fourteen sermons on the words, "We are saved by hope," from Rom. 8:24, and that he delivered seventeen on I John 4:20 and eighteen on John 3:6. The short text had taken over with a vengeance.

There has never been an adequate reason why the short text should have preempted the field. Nevertheless, there is no reason why a short text should not be used for many sermons. There are numerous epigrammatic statements which are literary units within themselves. Many of the sayings of Jesus fall within this category. There are other short passages which summarize in a remarkable way whole vistas of scripture.

Since it has been admitted, however, that there is no necessary

147

connection between a verse of scripture as numbered by Robert Etienne and his successors and a proper text for a sermon, one is confronted with the task of setting up the criteria for the choice of a text, including even a short text. This is to say, not every verse of scripture is an appropriate text for a sermon. Perhaps even a majority of separate verses should be disqualified as separate verses which could serve as texts for sermons. How, then, are we to locate the short passages which may be properly chosen as bases for sermons and legitimately used as texts in the proper sense of the term?

## Criteria for the Choice of a Text

*Context.* We have noted more than once throughout this book that it is necessary always to study a passage of scripture—long or short—in its contextual setting. I should like to say now that the text should not only be developed contextually, but that it should also be chosen contextually.

Take a familiar example from Ps. 46:10, "Be still, and know that I am God." This has often attracted the eyes of Christian preachers because of the first two words, which are read as an exhortation to silence, even to the time of prayer. The sermon is developed then as an attack upon our noisiness and our busy-ness and as a setting forth of the attractions of quietude. A reading of the entire psalm would have prevented the choice of that text from such a standpoint in the very beginning. The psalm is devoted to a presentation of a social catastrophe of such dimensions that it threatens to engulf the entire life of Israel. It is a historical earthquake: "The nations rage, the kingdoms totter." Kings, generals, armies in conquering might terrify the hearts of the Jews. In such a situation the psalmist calls attention to the King of kings who is sovereign over all nations and who brings all history into judgment. Let the Jews turn to this

General, finding their refuge and strength in him. Now we need the entire verse of which we quoted only the first third:

> Be still, and know that I am God.
> I am exalted among the nations,
> I am exalted in the earth!

James Moffatt translates this verse as follows:

> "Give in," he cries, "admit that I am God,
> high over the nations, high over the world."

The words "Be still" in the RSV mean "surrender," or as the ASV says in a marginal reading, "Let be!"

The sermon that results from this reading will be very different from the one that focuses in isolation upon a prayer retreat from the noise and activity of the world. This sermon requires a bold penetration into the very heart of the social hurricane, to the very citadel of history where God reigns, as at the eye of the storm.

*Centrality.* I have before me as I write an entire book containing nothing but quoted "text"—verses and fractions of verses—showing young ministers what to preach. There are more than two thousand of these texts. It would not be difficult to bring the number up to five thousand. The net result of trying to preach on all of these would be to pulverize and trivialize the gospel, for the majority of these texts are found on the margins of the biblical landscape and not at the center. Some, as quoted, are read more in the light of the preconceptions of the one choosing them than in the light of the scriptures; thus as quoted and understood these do not belong within the biblical landscape at all.

A text, to merit the attention of a minister for a week and

of a whole congregation for a half hour, should be central to the biblical revelation. Some knowledge of biblical theology will be essential to the choice. What are the characteristic and essential biblical ideas? John Knox helps us to answer this question in a brief list, not intended to be exhaustive, but which is nevertheless highly indicative:

The transcendence, the holiness, the power and sovereignty, the love of God; his demand of ethical righteousness; his judgment upon sin; man's creaturehood, his plight as a sinner; his need of forgiveness and release; the meaning of Christ as the actual coming of God into our history with the help we need; the availability of reconciliation and redemption, of life, joy, and peace, in the new community of the Spirit which God created through Christ and into which we can enter upon the sole condition of penitence and faith.[1]

The text for a sermon should adumbrate one or more of the central themes of the Bible.

*Balance.* A third criterion for the choice of a text is balance in the emphasis it makes. This should be considered both internally and relationally.

Internally, a text should present both the gift of God and the response of man. It should contain both judgment and grace. Even the Ten Commandments do not come upon us as sheer demand. They are framed in the love of God showing itself in an act of deliverance: "I am the Lord your God, who brought you out of the land of Egypt, out of the house of bondage" (Exod. 20:2). God takes the initiative through his unmerited gift of freedom; the commandments grow out of the resulting covenant between this God of liberation and a grateful people.

Kyle Haselden, editor of *The Pulpit,* from his vantage point

[1]John Knox, *The Integrity of Preaching* (Nashville: Abingdon, 1957), p. 19.

as a reader of thousands of contemporary sermons, has recently endeavored to summarize the elements essential to a genuine biblical sermon. He concludes that there are three such elements: "Man's Peril, God's Promise, and God's Act." [2] A few quotations will show his meaning: They are simply the ingredients of any biblical sermon.

We can therefore make three definite and conclusive statements about good preaching. First, it always sounds the note of warning. Subtly or bluntly it raises a signal over the Peril or over some aspect of the Peril. It sounds the alarm; it cries, "Danger, look out, beware"; it puts one on guard. If the sermon fails to do so, it is not faithful to the human situation; for the vulnerable life of man is immersed in a sea of troubles. If the sermon fails to sound the warning, it is not faithful to the listener: he is in great and grave danger; his flesh and his spirit are in jeopardy; he is confronted not merely by a minor inconvenience but by a major tragedy; and someone must tell him so or he perishes. And alas, if the sermon, as too often happens, lulls the listener into a false sense of security, if it whispers to the listener "All's well" when the world about him falls apart and the world within him explodes, then the sermon is not faithful to itself. It is worse than a deceiver; it is a traitor. And if the sermon fails its function as a warning, it is not faithful to the God who sets his ministers as watchmen in the night. [3]

Haselden quickly interjects that warning is not threatening. He illustrates the difference by contrasting two signs: "Beware of the dog!" which is a warning, and "Trespass, and we'll set our dogs on you!" which is a threat. A messenger of God warns; he does not threaten.

---

[2] These elements are not to be confused with sermon structure or outline.
[3] Kyle Haselden, *The Urgency of Preaching* (New York: Harper & Row, 1963), p. 43.

We are ready to make our second definite and conclusive statement about good preaching. The good sermon always presents the Promise over against the Peril. . . .

To say that God addresses his Promise to our total earthly condition—to all the glory and the wretchedness of our personal and our common life—is simply to declare the truth of the gospel. The Promise is God's universal and sufficient gift of his will, his love, and his power through his Son to needful man in all his conditions.[4]

Finally, we move to the third definite and conclusive statement about good preaching. The third element is God's Act:

If, then, the good sermon warns men of the threatening Peril and declares to them the assured Promise, it must also proclaim the Alterant operating decisively between the two. . . .

Indeed, what else do we have to offer men who dawdle between the pigsty on one side and their Father's home on the other? We are not sociologists, psychologists, or political scientists; we are proclaimers of the redeeming and reconciling act of God in Jesus Christ for the whole fabric of the human experience. However many ways we may need to turn to the sermon so that it penetrates the curtains men draw against it, however wide the application, this is the good news we proclaim to men: that "God was in Christ reconciling the world unto himself" and that "there is therefore now no condemnation for those who are in Christ Jesus." [5]

The text should be a door to this internal balance of the whole gospel for each sermon. Though many texts when considered as self-contained units may not refer explicitly to "Man's Peril, God's Promise and God's Act," all do so if they are considered contextually. Obviously, some texts are better doors to this total context than others.

[4] *Ibid.*, pp. 55-56.
[5] *Ibid.*, p. 62.

Not only should texts be balanced internally; they should also be balanced in relation to each other. This calls for some plan of preaching which will spread the selection of texts over Gospel and Epistles, Law, Prophets, and Writings. However this planning is done, it will stand in sharp contrast to the catch-as-catch-can method of choosing texts by whim and by hunch. It will rest in some program of biblical study which deals with biblical wholes—the books of scripture, ruling biblical ideas, or the phases of the Christian year, perhaps all three. This is not to say that "texts which choose you" almost as if they had a will of their own are to be rejected. It is simply to say that a minister needs to survey his preaching in year-long perspectives, both in prospect and in retrospect, to make sure that he is not habitually neglecting vast tracts of scripture and whole areas of Christian teaching.

Context, centrality, and balance—these three criteria for the choice of a text are indispensable to good biblical preaching. Consider next the development of a text into a sermon.

## Developing a Textual Sermon

It seems unnecessary here to follow the pattern of the other chapters in Part II of this book, i.e., to select a specific text and run it through the steps involved in making a sermon. Suffice it to say that each step is as important for a short text as for a longer one. The text must be selected so as to make sure that it is a proper biblical unit. It should be studied in its context, subjected to careful exegesis in the original tongues and in several versions. It should be considered from the standpoint of the student's own personal involvement in its truth. It should be paraphrased, its aim stated, its proposition written—all in the student's own words. And it should be submitted to the creative brooding which will permit the genuine growth of a

153

sermon. These steps, essential to any biblical sermon, are no less essential for a sermon on a short text.

Assuming the importance of the process just summarized and taking it for granted in this chapter, let us consider some of the aberrations of textual preaching to be avoided.

*Eisegesis*—reading an unintended meaning into a text. The familiar text from the KJV, "Study to shew thyself approved unto God, a workman that needeth not to be ashamed, rightly dividing the word of truth" (II Tim. 2:15) is often interpreted as an admonition to Bible study. A closer look at "study" and at "the word of truth" will dissolve that particular sermon into thin air. As to "study," the ASV had already translated the term "Give diligence," and the RSV removes all doubt as to the inherent meaning by translating, "Do your best to." The implication of a student bending over a book is obviously not intended.

This is further established when it is seen that "the word of truth" refers not to the written or printed Bible but to the word of the gospel. This is made quite explicit by Col. 1:15 and Eph. 1:13, where both phrases appear in apposition. The neat "rightly dividing" of the KJV becomes "rightly handling" in the RSV, and "driving a straight furrow" in the NEB. A contextual consideration will show that this diligent stewardship of the gospel as seen by the writer of II Timothy involves guarding it (1:14), preaching it (1:8), following it (1:13), and suffering for it (2:3). Obviously, eisegesis yields a much poorer sermon than proper exegesis will supply.

The words of the Bible in an English version should always be scrutinized. It is so easy to read surface meanings which are more in the eyes of the beholder than in the mind of the original author.

*Motto*—using a text not as the source of the ideas of the

sermon but as a point of departure for the minister's own development of a topic which he has in mind. In actual development such a text is often appended as an afterthought. What happens is that a man gets up a sermon on a purely topical basis but, being loath to present it as his own ideas, he "will bless it and approve it with a text," as Shakespeare said, "hiding the grossness with fair ornament."

But even if he starts with the words of a text, a man may use them as scarcely more than a convenient motto to sound a theme. Actually this method exploits a text and more often than not distorts it. I have before me an example of a sermon on a fraction of John 17:3, "This is eternal life." The full text is, "And this is eternal life, that they know thee the only true God, and Jesus Christ whom thou hast sent." It is a part of Jesus' high priestly prayer. As used in the Fourth Gospel, "eternal life" is the equivalent of the Synoptic "kingdom of God" and is synonymous with the Johannine "abundant life." Yet the author of the sermon that I have before me wanted to discuss death and life after death. In his actual sermon he is more dependent upon "and life everlasting" from the Apostles' Creed than upon his supposed text. If the author of the sermon wanted a biblical text he might better have turned to I Cor. 15:19 or II Cor. 5:1, where the main concern of the scripture is closer to the main concern of the sermon.

The score against a general practice of using motto texts consists of several counts. If engaged in by young ministers, it allows them to perpetuate a shallow knowledge of scripture without compelling them to deepen it. At the same time it may lull them into the delusion that they are actually doing biblical preaching when they are really proclaiming nothing more than cultural values which necessarily are imperfectly permeated by biblical ideas. Moreover, they are using the text as its masters

155

rather than serving the text as its ministers. The distinction is subtle but by no means insignificant.

The casual use of a text as motto, to cite one more count against it, most often robs the preacher of a better sermon in order to yield a poorer one. The sermon is there, waiting in the passage, but the hurried, preoccupied eye of the preacher glides over it without seeing it. There is a concreteness in the passage that would have saved him from abstractness, a fullness that would have delivered him from thinness of ideas.

An earlier discussion in this chapter touched on Ps. 46:10. I now return to this verse, recently used in my hearing as a motto for a sermon on "Creative Quietude." The sermon started out by demonstrating that we are not still—we are frantically busy and noisily talkative. It moved on to the effect of this restlessness and talkativeness—we miss the meaning of other people and we miss secret spiritual insights. The third main point called attention to the benefits of being still; by ordering our lives and practicing the stewardship of our thoughts we may come to know God. This sermon was highly topical, also quite abstract. As can be seen, the text, though often sounded throughout the sermon, was not really consulted. It was used, not served, by the preacher.

What insights might have guided that man to a better sermon, if he had stopped to really look at the text which he used so casually? As it was, he devoted his time to a discussion of the first two words, "Be still," which were misread. A division of the text into three parts with fairly equal attention to each would have been far more fruitful. The words "be still," as previously shown, mean "give in!" This involves a kind of surrender, a shift in loyalties and in perspective upon current history. Seen from one point of view the catastrophic events of the international scene with its wars and rumors of wars could cause nothing but terror. The text calls for an about-face and a new perspective. The words "and know" become revealing when it is seen that the word for "know" is from the Hebrew *yadha* (ידע) , which is also the word for sexual intercourse. This is an intimate kind of knowing—knowing by experience as against knowing by reason, debate, or speculation. It points to the God that the psalmist meets in his worship at the temple in Jerusalem, to the God he and his fathers have met in the many deliverances of the past from pharaohs and emperors now sleeping in the dust; Israel had lived from spiritual resources through the bankruptcy of many empires. It points to the psalmist's intuitive knowledge of the intimate presence of God and his unseen armies—refuge in strength, very present help in trouble. The words "I am God" affirm the real sovereignty within history. We more frequently act as if pharaoh, or Caesar, or the current dictator were God; or if we allow God to exist we grant him no dominion on earth in the affairs of nations.

*Proof text*—using a text to silence opposition and compel consent. Such preaching is inconsistent with the view of the Bible espoused in this book. It inheres in a literalistic, even legalistic belief in the plenary, verbal inspiration of the Bible which has been crowded out for most educated people by a larger, living Bible. This kind of preaching uses the Bible not as "a searchlight to be thrown upon a shadowed spot," but as a bludgeon to gain mastery. It degrades faith to credulity, debases gospel into law, and turns our Heavenly Father into a celestial dictator. Since God does not break and enter a human life, but always stands at the door and knocks, it is unworthy of God's ministers to be less respectful of human freedom and of the rights of human reason and consent. The truths of scripture will come to the hearer as insight or they will not come at all in their biblical dimension. If they are accepted on the authority of the scribes and the preachers alone, they will make slaves and not free men; they will prolong the spiritual infancy of those who are thus enslaved.

The habit of authoritarian preaching is so deeply engrained that it may persist in form long after its soul has departed. Therefore we need to be on guard lest we "speak as the scribes" and lose the true authority of the liberating word which we rightfully declare.

Short biblical texts will probably continue to dominate preaching for a long time to come. When their selection is guided by due consideration for context, centrality, and balance, and their development is guarded against eisegesis, superficiality, and authoritarianism, their use is not only to be trusted but encouraged. Their short, epigrammatic phrases stick like burrs to the memory, and (to change the figure) verse by verse, like stone upon stone, build up a citadel of faith in the lives of all who hear and recall them.

# 10

## Preaching on a Psalm

"Through the Psalter we can look into the heart of all the saints," Martin Luther said. Here are all the ranges and colors of human emotion known to honest religion, from the loftiest praise of God to the bitterest denunciation of enemies, and all the way from the ecstatic embrace of God's overwhelming presence to the abyss of his absence.

Writers of hymns and makers of sermons are drawn to the psalter as bees are drawn to a field of clover. The heavenly nectar is there for the taking—or so it seems at first glance. Nevertheless, what minister has not been captured by a psalm, only to be defeated and humiliated in his attempt to turn it into a sermon? Poetry which soars, when treated in our halting words limps and staggers along a dusty trail of dead prose. Or authentic poetry flies away into the fantasy and sentimentality of bogus emotion. It is not easy to preach an authentic sermon on a psalm.

How, then, shall we go about it?

### Interpreting a Psalm

(1) It is important to remember that a psalm belongs primarily to the realm of emotion rather than to the realm of logical thought. The analysis, categorization, and argumentation

which are so essential to discursive reasoning are broken tools for the opening of a psalm. The psalm will not open when it is thus attacked, but only when it is warmed in the heat and bathed in the light of our own sunlike emotions. Just as a pastor will fail in counseling if he asks, "What are this man's ideas, and what arguments shall I use to change his mind?" so will he miss the meaning of a psalm if he dissects it as a theological document. The theology is there, but more as a presupposition than as a statement; and it is all the while secondary. Therefore, just as an effective pastor must listen for the feelings of his counselee, asking, "What is he saying emotionally?" so he must listen to the feelings of the psalmist. Thus he will be able to enter the feelings of the personal and interpersonal world and deal with persons, not merely with impersonal ideas.

(2) It is, however, but a short distant from emotion to emotionalism or sentimentality. Genuine emotion is the feeling which is appropriate to an idea or an experience—it is the power of captivation in an experience or idea, and it derives from being fully present to an experience or an idea. Like the rising of the sun, it begins as light, then glows with warmth. Genuine emotion is not emotionally generated; it is, rather, personal response to reality as it claims us. Emotionalism and sentimentality, on the contrary, are feeling for the sake of the feeling itself. Emotionalism is a subjective orgy. Like a house afire, it begins in heat and smoke, then bursts into self-destructive flame. The psalter is a book of full and unashamed emotion, but there is not a single sentimental line in it.

This means that the preacher must be on guard against becoming snagged on the beauty of expression in a psalm, lest he never pass through the beautiful language to the bedrock experience which generated such language. If he starts with glowing heart and clouded mind, he will soon burn out, like a Fourth of July skyrocket. Do you recall those occasions on which you were so carried on the wings of the anthem before the sermon that you tried to begin the sermon itself on those same emotional heights, only to end in a dismal morass of blind feelings? A sermon must soar, but it must have a launching pad on the solid earth. It must go into orbit, but it cannot *start* two hundred miles above the earth.

(3) There follows a necessary implication for the reliving of the psalm, without which there can be no true sermon upon it. It is that the preacher must find beneath the beauty of language the solid reality of religious experience, at once the psalmist's and his own. A man who has never been in the abyss of despair over his own guilty failures can never possibly grasp the meaning of psalm 130:

> Out of the depths I cry to thee, O Lord!
>   Lord, hear my voice!
> Let thy ears be attentive
>   to the voice of my supplications!
> If thou, O Lord, shouldst mark iniquities,
>   Lord, who could stand?

Only one who has writhed in the agony of God's absence—not the general absence of an impersonal universe, but the personal abandonment of a God who has deserted *him*—can know the meaning of psalm 22:

> My God, my God, why hast thou forsaken me?
>   Why art thou so far from helping me, from
>     the words of my groaning?
> O my God, I cry by day, but thou dost not answer;
>   and by night, but find no rest.

Perhaps our religious experience is too elemental, too shallow, to match the profundities of the psalter. Certainly it is for some of the psalms. The psalmist paid for his truths in the coin of persecution, imprisonment, and exile; we who have never suffered a day's inconvenience for our convictions do not pick up his truth like pebbles on the beach. We are like children in the kindergarten who have yet to learn the alphabet trying to decipher the book of Job. We are far too immature for some psalms; we can no more reach their meanings than an infant stretching at full height can reach a doorknob. If we are wise we will leave these psalms for the future when, hopefully, we have grown up to them.

The forgoing observations, three in number, provide a fundamental orientation. They give a state of mind essential to the reliving of a psalm. To these must be added some structural rules for the psalm as a literary type:

(4) As Hebrew poetry, the psalms use parallelism of lines to produce a rhythm of thought. There are three main types of parallelism in the psalms, as in all Hebrew poetry. The first and most common is synonymous parallelism. The second line repeats the thought of the first line, as in the two parallels that follow:

> Save me, O God, by thy name,
>    and vindicate me by thy might.
> Hear my prayer, O God;
>    give ear to the words of my mouth (Ps. 54:1-2).

The words of the second line of each verse are different from the first line, but the thought is synonymous; it is a repeated idea.

The second type is antithetical parallelism, in which the second line stands opposed to the first. It is more common in the proverbs, but it also appears in the psalms:

> Better is a little that the righteous has
>    than the abundance of many wicked.

162

For the arms of the wicked shall be broken;
but the Lord upholds the righteous (Ps. 37:16-17).

The third type is synthetic parallelism or developing parallelism. The second line, and perhaps succeeding lines, develops the thought of the first line:

Come, behold the works of the Lord,
how he has wrought desolations in the earth (Ps. 46:8).

These three fundamental types of parallelism are combined in various ways to produce strophes and refrains.

(5) The psalms are subdivided not only into verses but these in turn are organized into strophes (not quite synonymous with stanzas in English poetry) and into refrains. The strophic structure of the psalms is easy to recognize in the RSV, since this version is printed with spaces between strophes. It is helpful to think that the development of the psalm takes a new turn with each new strophe. Therefore, the development of a psalm can be followed strophe by strophe; and each strophe may be summarized as a unity.

The strophic structure of psalm 32 may be studied as an example. This psalm contains six strophes. The first (vss. 1-2) extols the happiness of the man who has been forgiven his sins. The second (vss. 3-4) recalls the anguish and sickness of unconfessed sin. The third (vs. 5) recounts the writer's confession and forgiveness. The fourth (vss. 6-7) calls everyone to trust in God and offers personal testimony to God's delivering power. The fifth strophe (vss. 8-9) finds God addressing the writer in direct conversation, admonishing him to remain teachable. The sixth strophe (vss. 10-11) completes the psalm in a warning to the wicked which ends in a song of rejoicing for God's deliverance of the upright.

163

A strophe which becomes a refrain may be found in psalms 42 and 43 (which were originally one). This refrain occurs three times:

> Why are you cast down, O my soul,
>     and why are you disquieted within me?
> Hope in God; for I shall again praise him,
>     my help and my God.

The effect of such a refrain is reinforcement through repetition. It is confessional and liturgical in its power. Though the words of the refrain do not change, with each repetition they take on an increased cargo of meanings from the intervening strophes.

(6) The strophic structure of a psalm frequently lends itself as the best key to the structure of the sermon built on it. The movement of the psalm thus becomes the movement of the sermon, and since this movement in both cases is psychological rather than merely logical, it has gripping and holding power. It can transport the hearer from the point of initial involvement to a deeper level of faith.

### The Text

The text chosen for treatment in this chapter is psalm 139 in its entirety. It is cast in the form of private prayer. As such, it contrasts sharply with certain other psalms which are best voiced as hymns or corporate prayers of a congregation. The spokesman here is one man alone with his God. The mood, at least at the point of the psalm, is that shining in the lines of "Still, Still with Thee," Harriet Beecher Stowe's hymn:

> Alone with thee, amid the mystic shadows,
> The solemn hush of nature newly born;

Alone with thee in breathless adoration,
In the calm dew and freshness of the morn.

## The Text in Context

Aside from a few Aramaic words which would place the date of this psalm after the Babylonian exile, there is nothing to indicate a special historical situation. It is a timeless psalm speaking universally for man as man, a creature before the face of his Creator. The spokesman, as noted above, is a solitary individual. The form of his speech is private prayer, personal address to God. It rises from an intimate opening of the heart to God. The context therefore is not historical or sociological so much as psychological. It speaks for every man as creature before the face of his Creator, Judge, and Redeemer.

## Spelling Out Some Textual Meanings

I. First strophe (vss. 1-6). *O God, you know me through and through.* What I know of God is not the question here. I am not the knower, but the known. God knows me intimately and exhaustively. There is nothing that escapes his all-seeing gaze. There are opaque depths in me when I look introspectively into my own being; God's knowledge of me penetrates even these depths. I can conceal nothing. He knows it all.

(1) *Searched and known me:* Jeremiah expressed the same idea: "I the Lord search the mind and try the heart" (17:10). The search is thorough; nothing in my inner life escapes notice. (2) *Thou knowest:* the "thou" is emphatic: one might say, "Thou alone knowest." *When I sit down and when I rise up:* in other words, everything, every least little thing that I do—all my activities. *My thoughts:* refers not to ideas but to desires, disposition, and longings. *From afar:* might be "deep down" in modern parlance. (3) *Thou searchest out:* the force is to "sift" or "winnow"—"You thresh and winnow my doings."

165

*My path and my lying down:* Moffatt says, "walking or rest-ing." There is no time off from this scrutiny; it pierces even my leisure hours. *All my ways:* the implication is "all my dealings with other people." Moffatt says, "All my life . . . lies open."

(4) *Even before a word is on my tongue:* God knows the real intention behind my spoken words, all my concealed motives; and he knows this before I put it into words. (5) *Beset me behind and before:* the picture is that of a city surrounded and under armed siege. *Layest thy hand upon me:* "grabbed me" would be a less elegant way of saying the same thing; or "pinned me down." (6) *Too wonderful for me . . . high:* such knowl-edge simply overwhelms me; it is beyond my power to compre-hend it.

II. Second strophe (vss. 7-12). *I try but I cannot escape you.* Job complained of this unsleeping watch over his life (7:17-20). Why can't God leave me alone? There is nothing comforting in his all-seeing gaze. I much prefer the twilight of pleasant fictions about myself to the glaring truth of broad daylight. There may be days when my mood is, "O that I knew where I might find him, that I might come even into his presence," but that is not my present mood. All I want now is a place to hide from him, even for a little while.

(7) *Whither shall I . . . flee:* flight from God is my first reac-tion. I seek a refuge from this blinding light. "It is safe to say that a man who has never tried to flee God has never ex-perienced the God Who is really God. . . . A god whom we can easily bear, a god from whom we do not have to hide, a god whom we do not hate in moments, a god whose destruction we never desire, is not God at all, and has no reality," said Paul Tillich.[1] *Thy Spirit . . . thy presence:* God is spiritual

[1] *The Shaking of the Foundations* (New York: Charles Scribner's Sons, 1948), p. 42.

166

presence, absent nowhere. There is no place to hide from him. (8) *If I ascend to heaven:* outer space, high above the habitat of men. *If I make my bed in Sheol:* the netherworld, outside the domain of the living. Sheol was also "the grave." Tillich, commenting on this, wrote, "I am convinced that there is not one amongst us who has not at some time desired to be liberated from the burden of his existence by stepping out of it. And I know that there are some amongst us for whom this longing is a daily temptation." [2] (9) *If I take the wings of the morning:* this is flight into speed—the speed of the rising and setting sun—and it is also flight beyond the last human frontier—the farthest bounds of human habitation and achievement. "If I escape in speed, you arrive ahead of me. If I carve out a new frontier, you set up your claim long before me." (11) *Darkness . . . night:* Moffatt says, "If I say, 'The dark will screen me, night will hide me in its curtains.' " The night means rest, sleep, unconsciousness—escape and renewal. (12) *Darkness is as light with thee:* in the night watches when we see ourselves even more clearly than during the rush of the day, God sees still more keenly. And in the luminous insight of our dreams, his light showers upon us.

III. Third strophe (vss. 13-18) . *In every cell and fiber of my being, I am your handiwork; you are the life of my life.* Now the mood shifts. I begin to realize that God's knowledge of me is not an invasion of my privacy, for it is not the knowledge of an outsider or a stranger. It is a knowledge arising from the very power of being by which I was born and by which I live. It is knowledge preceded and surrounded by the gift of life in all its mystery and depth. Resentment and fright at being exposed are displaced by wonder and gratitude.

[2] *Ibid.,* pp. 40-41.

(13) *My inward parts:* the Hebrew word is "kidneys," meant to stand for all the vital organs of the body. It would be accurate to say, "For thou didst form my heart and lungs, my liver and my spleen, my kidneys and my digestive system." *Thou didst knit me together in my mother's womb:* through the mysterious processes of conception, gestation, and embryonic growth I came into this world; that is how God made me. The figure is the same with Job: "Thou didst clothe me with skin and flesh, and knit me together with bones and sinews." (14) *I praise thee:* wonder and gratitude have expelled resentment and fear. Whereas formerly I fled from God, now I take refuge in him. (15) *My frame was not hidden from thee:* God can see my skeleton, which I can never see. *When I was being made in secret:* in the womb of my mother. *Intricately wrought:* embroidered veins and arteries, according to one rabbi. *In the depths of the earth:* Plato in *The Republic* recounts an old Phoenician tale to the effect that children "were being formed and fed in the womb of the earth, where they themselves and their arms and appurtenances were manufactured; when they were completed, the earth, their mother, sent them up" (to be implanted in the womb of a human mother?). This is a poetic assertion of man's mystic bond with nature.[3] (16) *Thy eyes beheld my unformed substance:* my embryo. *In thy book . . . the days:* this is predestination, not as a dogma, but as an experience of the mystery of my own birth and being. I was made teleologically—with an inwrought purpose. The symbol of God's book for the living is found also in Ps. 69:28, Exod. 32:32-33, Mal. 3:16, and Dan. 12:1. (17, 18) *Thy thoughts . . . more than the sand. . . . When I awake:* the mood is that of reverie

[3] *The Republic,* III: 414, tr. by B. Jowett (New York: Random House, 1937), p. 124.

induced by awe and wonder at the countless points at which the power of the living God has touched and is touching my life. Or, "I count and count, until I fall asleep counting, without ever coming to the end." The marginal reading says, "Were I to come to the end I would still be with thee." God's care just for me, one solitary individual, is literally infinite.

IV. Fourth strophe (vss. 19-24). *My prayer against the wicked.*

*In the light of such intimate divine care, how I hate the wicked* (vss. 19-22). For the moment I forget my own earlier resentment of God's unsleeping gaze upon me. Swept up into grateful awe at the intricacy of God's creative, life-giving touch upon human life, I am suddenly incensed that anyone should defy God or lift himself up—by power derived from God himself—against God. If I could have my way, the psalmist says, I would kill all such people. Why doesn't God kill them? Oh, how I hate them!

This is an abrupt, jarring note in the psalm, but no less logical than the flight from God's presence in vss. 7-12. It is true to religious experience. A man who has once clearly seen God's patient benevolence becomes horrified at the effrontery of human malevolence; he wants it extirpated from the world. And, in an orgy of self-righteousness, he momentarily sees wickedness as other men's evil.

Notice the strong verbs of this strophe: *slay, defy, hate, loathe.* Here is righteous indignation at white heat. (21) *And do I not loathe them that rise up against thee?* Moffatt renders the verse: "Shall I not loathe these rebels?" [4]

*Alas! I must include myself in this prayer over the wicked! I myself constantly need thy judgment and your guiding mercy*

[4] Comment on individual verses is omitted; the general commentary is deemed sufficient.

(vss. 23-24). Still within the strophe which boils with hot indignation against wicked men, my mood suddenly turns home in penitence and contrition. My final petition is for the threshing of God's intimate judgment to be followed by his loving guidance. And my psalm ends as it begins, with one solitary individual—myself—alone before God's face.

(23) *Search me . . . try me:* I have already been searched and threshed (vs. 3), but whereas I fled from this testing at an earlier, less mature stage of my spiritual growth, now I welcome it because I so desperately need it. Only in the refiner's fire of God's blast furnace will my impurities be burned out and my true gold appear. *Know my heart:* what before was a torment is now a comfort. I who know myself so dimly am fully known and fully understood by the One who created me and loves me with an everlasting love. *Know my thoughts:* the word is different from *thoughts* in vs. 2, where it meant "intimate thoughts" (*rea*). Here it means "disquieting thoughts" (*sarrapim*); the term implies a branching out in two directions. "Try my double-mindedness, my limping between two opinions," seems to be the force of the petition. (24) *Any wicked way in me:* Moffatt says, "See if I am taking a wrong course." Samuel Terrien interprets, "any oppressive, harmful and hurtful tendency in me." A targum on the Masoretic text reads "way of idolatry." How subtly the rebel within asserts itself! How rigorous must be the search to uncover him! *And lead me in the way everlasting:* not immortality, but God's own well-established ways, as in Jer. 6:16:

> Stand by the roads, and look,
>    and ask for the ancient paths,
> where the good way is; and walk in it,
>    and find rest for your souls.

170

### Putting Yourself into the Text

This prayer, spoken in the first person singular, fits my lips as though individually made for them. Between the original author and myself there is no barrier of time and place. I am that man.

A reliving of the first two strophes can be done by way of an intimate biographical review. Perhaps you were like me, haunted in childhood by the great unblinking eye of God following me everywhere, even in the dark of my bed-chamber. (I had seen it in our huge family Bible.) It was an oppressive presence. Think of your own times of uneasy squirming under that gaze, relive the individual memories in which they lie embedded. Likewise, relive your many clever ruses, your attempted escapes from that all-seeing gaze—your flights into feverish activities, your attempted vacations from God, your retreats into sleep or laziness, your refuge in your own noble deeds, your burrowing under books and knowledge, your storming of heaven itself in the meritorious exploitation of prayer, Bible reading, and attendance upon religious rituals. Remember detail upon detail upon detail; pursue yourself running, step by step.

The reliving of the third strophe will require that you selectively focus your mind upon your own body and its processes, one organ at a time, one process at a time. Sit quietly, until you can hear your own heartbeat and feel the blood pulsing through your arteries. Now pay close attention to your breathing—the mystery by which the outside atmosphere becomes part of you, and inside wastes are exhaled to become part of the atmosphere again. Think of what you ate for breakfast, and how it is even now becoming your bone and blood and tissue. Close your eyes; imagine that you are blind and cannot see—that you will never see light of day again; now open your eyes and give thanks for the gift of sight. Stretch out your hand before you, command one finger to move, then another. Pinch yourself and feel the pain. Stand up and take a step; think what it would mean if that were your first step—or your last. (The meditation cannot be spelled out in detail here. Continue it for several minutes until you can say truthfully and gratefully, "I praise thee, for thou art fearful and wonderful. Wonderful are thy works!" Then go on to the two movements and moods of the final strophe, reliving each step autobiographically, deed by deed, thought by thought.)

## Finding the Internal Unity of the Psalm

*Aim:* To show the changing, maturing response of each man to God's omniscience, omnipresence, and omnificence when through these the living God comes intimately near.

*Proposition:* In the face of God's sovereign and intimate shaping of my life, how vain it is to flee, how necessary to welcome his judgment and pray for his grace!

## Uncovering the Dynamics of the Psalm

Conflict and movement surge through this psalm. Notice at least five fundamental rhythms:

(1) God watching me, piercing me through and through with his gaze: I, hedged in on every side, trapped as in a walled city under siege.

(2) I trying in headlong flight to escape him, frantically bolting into one hiding place after another: He, "the Hound of Heaven," with unhurrying pace, "majestic instancy" following after me and overtaking me at every turn.

(3) I feeling his living work of creation in my bones and my being, pumping in my blood, whispering in my breath, surging in digestion, singing in my nerves and brain: I again suddenly realizing how little I know of myself, I who am so fully known and cared for.

172

(4) My anger flashing out at those who use the power of life and breath given by God to rebel against God: My contrition rising as I recognize the rebellion within myself.

(5) I pleading for God's constant testing, and for his unfailing guidance.

### Précis

O Lord, you have ransacked my inner life; you know me through and through. You know everything I do—when I get up, when I go to bed, when I am at home, and when I go to the office. You read my mind. You thresh and winnow my doings, and all my dealings with people. You know what I am going to say before I say it, and you know my intention when I hide my secret thoughts behind my words. You have surrounded me and captured me. Such knowledge of my personal life completely overwhelms me.

You make me want to hide. But where shall I go to escape you? If I flee into space, you are there. If I flee into the grave, you are there. If I escape into speed, you arrive ahead of me. If I try to cover myself with darkness, you see me with cat's eyes. There *is* no hiding place.

You made me, every cell. You made my vital organs. You covered me with skin, and made my bones and muscles. How wonderful! You know every cubic inch of me. My skeleton was not hid from you when you made me and fashioned me so intricately—arteries and veins, nerves and brain—in the womb of Mother Earth. When I was an embryo, you saw me and looked after me. You knew beforehand all the days of my life. Oh, what a weight upon my little knowledge is such knowledge, O God! If I tried to count your thoughts merely about me, I would fall asleep counting. I would go on counting in my sleep, and when I awoke I would still be counting—and still within thy meticulous watchcare.

173

With all your power, in the face of all that you do for men, why do you allow wicked men to live? I would kill them! You even allow men to defy you using your own gift of power, to rise in rebellion against you! I hate, I loathe them. Your enemies have become my enemies. Let us crush them.

But wait! I am not that pure. There is evil in me too—crookedness, double-mindedness. Pour me into your blast furnace, O God, smelt out *my* impurities; refine me until you have the gold of me. Lead me into thy way of life.

### Brainstorming the Text

In this instance, much of the work of brooding has already been done. Therefore a brief comment will suffice. Francis Thompson's classic poem, "The Hound of Heaven," will come readily to mind for the second strophe of the psalm, as will Paul Tillich's sermon (in *The Shaking of the Foundations*), "The Escape from God."

Several hymns have been inspired by this psalm, chief among them Harriet Beecher Stowe's "Still, Still with Thee." Consider the opening stanzas of three other hymns from a century-old hymnal.

> Father of spirits! nature's God,
>   Our inmost thoughts are known to thee
> Thou, Lord, canst hear each idle word,
>   And every private action see.
>
> Lord, Thou hast searched and seen me through;
> Thine eye commands with piercing view
> My rising and my resting hours,
> My heart and flesh with all their powers.
>
> Lord, thou hast formed mine every part,
>   Mine inmost thought is known to thee;

Each word, each feeling of my heart,
Thine ear doth hear, thine eye doth see.

As I write, the "death of God" theology is the current agitation of the American religious scene. It should be noted that biblical writers are well acquainted with the God who hides himself (Isa. 45:15; Job 13:24; Ps. 44:24; 88:14; 89:46), the God who abandons his chosen, as with King Saul (I Sam. 16:14; 18:12; 28:15-16), and who makes himself inaccessible, as from Job (Job 23: 3, 8-9). This withdrawal of God into silence and emptiness is seemingly what happens whenever we try to grasp him as an object of human knowledge or utility. The absence of God, in that instance, is the presence of God's judgment upon us. He leaves us alone in our predicament. In all true experience of God's presence, the knowledge of God reverses subject and object, as Paul shows so swiftly in a famous passage: "Now that you have come to know God, or rather to be known by God" (Gal. 4:9). Scientific knowledge of God is and will always remain beyond our reach; for God, to be God, cannot become an object of knowledge or a power for us to exploit. In the same way he will always elude our arguments to establish his existence or nonexistence. And he will always remain the subject, the sovereign in the world of his creation, who knows and sees with piercing eyes, who wounds and heals with a surgeon's love, that we may be whole.

Sidney Lanier's "The Marshes of Glynn" will come to many minds as one appropriate expression of the intimate, personal way in which one may experience the presence of God.

As the marsh-hen secretly builds on the watery sod,
Behold I will build me a nest on the greatness of God:
I will fly in the greatness of God as the marsh-hen flies

IN THE BIBLICAL PREACHER'S WORKSHOP

> In the freedom that fills all the space 'twixt the
>     marsh and the skies:
> By so many roots as the marsh-grass sends in the sod
> I will heartily lay me a-hold on the greatness of God.

The rest of the poem is equally rewarding.

### Striking Through to Outline

The psalm's own movement, forming the paragraphing of the sections, "Spelling Out Some Textual Meaning" and "Uncovering the Dynamics of the Psalm" becomes the most natural avenue to the organization of the sermon. The outlines implicit in these sections need not be repeated here.

Another approach, perhaps too topical, divides the action of God from the response of man:

I. The action of God
   A. In omniscience
   B. In omnipresence
   C. In omnificence
II. The response of man
   A. In attempted escape
   B. In wonder and gratitude
   C. In hatred and evil
   D. In confession and penitence

A still further approach, more psychological, less impersonal, and also closer to the psalm's own mood and movement, avoids the third person and uses the more intimate *you* and *I:*

I. O God, when you come home to me personally in all your knowledge of me
   A. There is nothing in me that you do not see
   B. And I am so terrified that I try to escape from you

176

II. O God, when you overtake me with all your power
    A. I feel your creative touch in every cell of my body
    B. I respond in wonder and gratitude
    C. I hate all evil men who rebel against you, subverting your power to their wicked purposes
III. O God, when you overtake me with your patient goodness
    A. I discover my own deviousness
    B. I pray gratefully for thy continued testing of me
    C. I rely hopefully upon your continued guidance

### Naming the Sermon

Various possibilities suggest themselves: "The God Who Knows Me," "The God Who Believes in Me," "My God and I," "Still, Still with Thee," and Paul Tillich's title for his sermon on this entire psalm, "The Escape from God."

# 11

## Preaching on a Perplexing Passage

Certain passages of scripture seem to defy Christian interpretation. On first sight, at least, they are opaque to the Christian preacher. I refer not to texts which were broken in transmission and whose meaning is therefore murky, but to scriptures which appear to violate biblical values. Were it not for the fact that they are in the Bible they would be as acceptable as the tragedies of Aeschylus or the legendary exploits of Paul Bunyan. They vex us not because they are untrue to life but because they do not seem to ring true of a God who is just and merciful. In other words, they are readily acceptable as literature, so long as that literature is not considered revelatory. We can hear them as the cry of men, but as the word of God they confuse and baffle us.

To cite a few examples, what are we to do with the story of Jephthah's vow in Judg. 11:29-40? I once put that question to a continental Lutheran whose high doctrine of the word of God through preaching seemed equal to almost any challenge; scripture was not a locked box requiring a special key; its message was plain, needing only an obedient servant of the word. His reply was, "Honestly, I don't know." The sin of Achan in Josh. 7, when he violated *the ban* ("devoted thing") at Jericho and enriched himself by taking loot from the defeated city, was

178

certainly not praiseworthy; but Joshua's punishment of Achan for his sin—involving the slaughter of Achan's whole family and the destruction of all his livestock and property—looks positively wicked. How can it be read as revelatory of God's will? The sordid tale of the Levite's concubine and the sodomites of Gibeah in Judg. 19 is lurid; what can it possibly say about God? Can Samuel have been speaking for God when he commanded King Saul to undertake the slaughter of every last Amalekite (I Sam. 15:1-33)? By the standards of the Geneva Convention, this would be known as "the crime of genocide." Modern chapters of the same sort of thing include Hitler's effort "to solve the Jewish problem" by systematically murdering Jews on a mass scale. What touchstone of interpretation can make the act of Samuel good while the act of Hitler remains evil? And, to compound the perplexity, are we to approve when Samuel, in high indignation at Saul's disobedience, actually offered King Agag as a human sacrifice on the altar, first having chopped his body to pieces with his own hand (I Sam. 15:32-33)? Still another instance of many is the shocking incident of Exod. 4:24-26:

At a lodging place on the way the Lord met him [Moses] and sought to kill him. Then Zipporah took a flint and cut off her son's foreskin, and touched Moses' feet with it, and said, "Surely you are a bridegroom of blood to me!" So he let him alone. Then it was that she said, "You are a bridegroom of blood," because of the circumcision.

It is not our purpose to be exhaustive. Perhaps the problem has been sufficiently illustrated in the examples already listed. What is the preacher to do about such passages?

There is a legitimate scholarly approach to them which falls in the realm of science and history. These strands of literature are fascinating to the cultural anthropologist, the form critic, and the historian of religions. That is to say, the study of these passages has its place in academic communities, but does it belong in the pulpit? Certainly the legitimate approaches just mentioned do not approximate the purpose of the editors of the Bible or the congregation of Israel which preserved them in oral tradition. Such scriptures were preserved, transmitted, edited, and offered as parts of redemption history; they were offered in faith and are meant to be read in faith.

Two obstacles stand between us and such reading-in-faith. These are our own unrecognized presuppositions and the unrecognized presuppositions of the original authors or storytellers. We have to divest ourselves of the first, but invest ourselves with the second. Take *the ban* (or "devoted thing") as illustrated both in the capture and sack of Jericho and in the defeat of the Amalekites (Josh. 6 and I Sam. 15). A natural assumption for us to make in reading about either of these acts of ancient warfare is that the victors should have treated the prisoners of war by the rule of humane warfare as laid down in the Geneva Convention. But the Geneva Convention was centuries in the future at the time of the events with which we have to deal. The humane treatment of war prisoners was not even an option for them at the time. Vanquished warriors could then expect one of two fates—execution or enslavement; no third alternative presented itself. When *the ban* treated a captured city or people as a sacrifice to be offered up to God, the force of the commandment was not only to make the engagement a holy war, but even more deeply, it was to eliminate all motives of greed and self-interest from the fighting men. This was a cause so holy (so went the view of the times) that no one must be permitted to enrich himself by taking booty to be added to his property or captives who could become his domestic slaves. When Achan and Saul violated *the ban* they did so from no humane considerations whatever; they simply could not resist their own greed and self-glorification. Achan threw over community responsibilities and religious duty for personal gain; it was an anarchistic act of pure greed. No nation, surely no chosen nation, could erect its house on such shifting sand.

Only one more thing is needed. This is the opposite of scholarly profundity. It is a kind of childlike naïveté which sees the story in simple terms and as containing the clues to its own meaning. It is, in fact, possible to look too hard and too deep for the meaning of such passages. Less sophisticated eyes may see it at once. It may be there on the surface in plain view. Once we are over the notion that it is unworthy of God to kill a man, for example, the gory incident from the fourth chapter of Exodus quoted above readily yields us a meaning: The thing that saved Moses' life was the circumcision of his son. When it is remembered that circumcision is the seal of a special covenant with God, the meaning is obvious. Without progeny who bear the mark of the covenant, Moses, giver of the Torah, was dead.

Having lingered for this preliminary word about perplexing passages in general, we turn in the balance of this chapter to one particular passage, the testing of Abraham in Gen. 22:1-19.

## The Text

Gen. 22:1-19 tells how Abraham set out to obey God's command to offer up Isaac as a human sacrifice and how both he and Isaac were rescued from the ordeal by the substitution of a ram. Variously labeled "The Testing of Abraham," "The Ordeal of Isaac," and "The Sacrifice of Isaac," the passage is perplexing on two major counts: (1) The apparent cruelty of God. How can we possibly think of God as ever requiring such a barbarous thing as the slaying of a human being in an act of divine worship? (2) The evident inconsistency of God. Since God had promised through Isaac to make the descendants of

Abraham into a numerous people, why does he now appear to annul that promise completely by commanding the killing of Isaac? On both counts—if we are honest about it—the passage violates our religious sensitivities.

### The Text in Context

Many strands are woven together to make up the narrative in the middle chapters of Genesis. To get the narrative context of the passage now under study it is necessary to isolate a single strand—that dealing with the fulfillment of God's promise to Abraham through Isaac. We should go back to Gen. 12:1-3, "Now the Lord said to Abram, 'Go from your country and your kindred and your father's house to the land that I will show you. And I will make of you a great nation . . . and by you all the families of the earth will bless themselves.' " The fulfillment of that promise required that Abraham should have a son; but no son was forthcoming. Year after year passed, but Sarah and Abraham remained childless. Determined to have an heir, Abraham adopted a slave, Eliezer of Damascus, as a son, meanwhile complaining to God, "Behold, thou hast given me no offspring; and a slave born in my house will be my heir" (Gen. 15:3) . God soon blocked this road, however: " 'This man shall not be your heir; your own son shall be your heir.' And he brought him outside and said, 'Look toward heaven, and number the stars, if you are able to number them.' Then he said to him, So shall your descendants be' " (Gen. 15:4-5) . Though the promise of a son of his own was renewed, the fulfillment of the promise was again pushed into the indefinite future.

As the years wore on, this promise wore thin. Again Abraham took matters into his own hands; he would have a son by Hagar, a slave girl. This attempt was also frustrated. Though Ishmael was born to Hagar, Abraham was forced to put mother and son out of his house and to relinquish all prospects of progeny through that line (Gen. 16:1-16; 21:9-21). The son God wanted had to be Sarah and Abraham's. With advancing age, however, Sarah passed beyond the years of child-bearing. The promise appeared to be doomed. When finally it was renewed, Sarah laughed at the ridiculousness of it (Gen. 18:9-15). But when at last Isaac was born, the true son of Sarah and Abraham, their joy knew no bounds (Gen. 21:1-8).

Isaac's infancy and childhood are passed over in silence; when next he appears he is on the threshold of young manhood. The bond between father and son had grown into a precious thing. The tenderness of this affection is well represented in Gen. 22:2, "Your son, your only son Isaac, whom you love." Now falls the cruel command, "Take your son . . . and offer him there as a burnt offering upon one of the mountains." Promises long delayed and often postponed, affection made sweet by years of waiting—all are dashed to the ground in one devastating word. The Letter to the Hebrews preserves the tension of the long delay of parenthood: "Therefore from one man, and him as good as dead, were born descendants as many as the stars of heaven and as the innumerable grains of sand by the seashore" (Heb. 11:12).

In addition to the narrative strand relating to son and progeny for Abraham, we need the biblical perspective upon human sacrifice. This revolting cultic rite was observed by Israel's geographical neighbors, and came under the denunciation of biblical writers. (See Lev. 20:2; Deut. 12:30-31; II Kings 16:3; 17:31; 23:10; Ps. 106:37-38; Jer. 7:30-32; 19:3-5; Ezek. 16:20-21.)

The moral weight upon Israel of this costly devotion of neighboring foreigners to their gods would have been little short of overwhelming: "Do we love our God the less because we withhold this last measure of devotion?" Besides, such costly acts of devotion appeared in early Israelite eyes to have enormous

183

potency, as witness their reaction to the king of Moab's sacrifice of his son in II Kings 3:27. The Indications are that the Israelites themselves succumbed to the allurements of the rite: "You shall not give any of your children to devote them by fire to Molech, and so profane the name of your God" (Lev. 18:21). Such a prohibition would have been unnecessary unless some Israelites were actually engaging in child sacrifice, as is shown by II Kings 23:10 and Jer. 32:35. The valley of Hinnom acquired its evil meaning from the frequent burning of children on its altars. The cultic practice of redeeming the firstborn assumed an earlier practice of offering them up. (See Num. 3:11-13, 40-51; 18:15-16; and Exod. 13:1-2, 11-16.) There were those in Israel's early history who answered "Yes!" to the question later phrased by Micah,

> Shall I give my first-born for my transgression,
> the fruit of my body for the sin of my soul?
> (Mic. 6:7)

Though it is now impossible for us to suppose that God ever required human sacrifice, Abraham lived in a culture which presupposed it. The sacerdotal slaughter of young men and women and even of little children as an act of piety was a gruesome fact of the times. And it continued for centuries beyond the time of Abraham. The remarkable thing is not that Israel succumbed to this practice now and then but that she outgrew it or resisted it so firmly.

### Spelling Out Some Textual Meanings

*Gen. 22:1. God tested Abraham:* here the writer states the purpose of the narrative. It is to see whether Abraham's obedience to God is thorough; God requires devotion without reservation. Does Abraham have it? The notion that God could test the faithfulness of his people occurs elsewhere in the Old Testament. (See Deut. 13:3; Judg. 2:22; and Job 1:6-12.) The reader here gets advance notice that God does not really desire the sacrifice of Isaac; he only wants to be assured that the father of his chosen people will keep the covenant unconditionally. The Anchor Bible's captioning of the narrative as "The Ordeal of Isaac" is, therefore, ill-advised. The name of the story is properly "The Testing of Abraham."

*Gen. 22:2. Take your son . . . and offer him:* in addition to breaking a father's heart, God commanded something completely contradictory and incomprehensible. Isaac was the only link to a progeny as numerous as the stars of the heavens and the sands of the sea, which would fulfill the promise of God (Gen. 15:5-6) . In obeying God, Abraham had left Ur of the Chaldees and Haran, thus cutting himself off from his past; now it appeared that God was asking him to cut himself off from the future as well.

*Gen. 22:2 The land of Moriah:* not to be identified with Mount Moriah, though II Chr. 3:1 assumes that. The Septuagint and Syriac versions disagree. The place is unknown to us.

*Gen. 22:3-8.* The remarkable restraint of the narrative builds up the emotional pressure of these and succeeding verses by telling only what is said and what is done without any report on the inner thoughts of Abraham or Isaac. The economy of words corresponds to a mood too full for words. Every detail is a wound in the breast of the loving father of the innocent young man. Three days of journeying, mostly in oppressive silence, proves the steadfastness of Abraham's obedience; it persists through nights and days; it does not waver. *God will provide:* The Hebrew verb is the verb for "see," in the sense of "see to it." In succeeding verses a Hebrew wordplay develops: vs. 8, *elohim yereh* (אלהים יראה) , "God will see to it." Vs. 12, *Ki yere elohim*

(בִּי־יִרָא אֱלֹהִים), "because you fear God." Vs. 14, *Yahweh yireh* (יהוה יראה), "Yahweh will provide," or "Yahweh appears." The refrain that is set up by this wordplay surely must be intended to make and emphasize a point.

*Gen. 22:9-14.* Details here, as in the previous section, are sharp, yet restricted. It is a story in which the deeper meanings appear between the lines and beneath the words. *I know that you fear God:* as we have seen, this is a part of the wordplay. "Fear" as given here means reverent obedience—faithfulness. It is not so much an emotion as a way of life. In the wordplay, the effect is to show how God's faithfulness answers the faithfulness of Abraham.

*Gen. 22:15-19.* The story is complete without this paragraph, which is given evidently to connect the narrative into the promise of Gen. 15:5-6. It is paradoxical that Abraham gets the fulfillment of the promise only through his willingness to surrender it. Because he did not withhold his only son from God, he is now to have not only a son, but, "children's children" through countless generations, and "by your descendants shall all the nations of the earth bless themselves."

### Putting Ourselves into the Text

The point of fascination in the narrative for the modern reader is human sacrifice. It is easy to get hung up there and miss the deeper point. The passage is neither a protest against human sacrifice nor a condoning of it. It merely uses such sacrifice (a familiar practice in the patriarchal world) as the most extreme kind of test imaginable to show Abraham's unwavering faithfulness to God. It is a radical test of Abraham's obedience. As Gerhard von Rad says, the narrative "concerns something much more frightful than child sacrifice. It has to do with a road out into Godforsakenness on which Abraham does not

186

know that God is only testing him." [1] Abraham had cut himself off from his past when he obeyed God's summons to leave his native land and his kinfolk for an unknown promised land. Now God asked Abraham to give up the future which had lured him and to obey even when obedience appeared to be self-destroying. Abraham's earlier obedience in forsaking homeland and kinfolk did not earn him any legal claim upon God's rewards; it did not exempt him from the hazards of living on a spiritual frontier where he could lose everything.

If we look at Isaac—and at Israel as descended from him—we see this people as given up to God and as possessing its life now only through God's grace. "That is to say, it [Israel] could base its existence in history not on its own legal titles as other nations did, but only on the will of Him who in the freedom of his grace permitted Isaac to live." [2] This is a secondary interest of the narrative, perhaps an inescapable one. But it is clear that the primary interest is focused upon Abraham and the apparently contradictory nature of God's claims upon him.

Making our identification with Abraham, pioneer of faith, we are asked to walk by faith and not by sight. Putting aside motives of religious utility and spiritual guarantees, we are told to venture on our faith even at extreme cost, when obedience appears utterly self-destroying. As Alfred North Whitehead put it, "A man has not found his religion until he has found that for which he will risk and hazard his all." Only in this way can we be dealing with an ultimate concern. The test of ultimacy does not come upon us in general terms, however; it appears, dated and addressed, in the midst of domestic and business affairs, in the midst of the very concrete events that compose our

---

[1] *Genesis: A Commentary,* tr. by John H. Marks (Philadelphia, Westminster Press, 1961) , p. 239.

[2] *Ibid.,* p. 240.

days. It can involve vocational choices, business and political decisions, and social sacrifices in which the will of God stands clearly over against our wishes. This losing of life in order to find it is of the essence of faith; if we are to take faith seriously there is no realm of existence that is off limits to the radical claim of God.

## Finding the Internal Unity of the Text

*Aim:* To show the life of faith as a life beyond human calculation; as an absurd, life-destroying leap of trust in obedience to God.

*Secondary aim:* To show how God requires the giving up of family and other idolatry in the interest of full loyalty to him.

*Proposition:* Abraham obeyed God when obedience seemed against every promise of God and every counsel of self-interest and reason; and when he had met the test, God gave him back all he had threatened and more. Make this contemporaneous and it becomes: We are called to obey God even when obedience seems against every promise of God and every counsel of self-interest and reason; and if we meet that test, God will provide for us in ways past our reckoning.

*Key verses:* "After these things God tested Abraham. . . . So Abraham called the name of that place The Lord will provide" (Gen. 22:1, 14) .

## Uncovering the Dynamics of the Text

*The tensions:* Love of family versus love of God. The promise of God versus God's destroying demand. Abraham's faith versus his postponed hope and his despair.

*The movement:* The shattering command. The long, torturous journey in obedience. The tender exchange between father

188

and son. The near sacrifice of Isaac. The ram caught in the thicket. The rescue of Isaac and Abraham. The renewal of the promise.

## Brainstorming the Text

The underlying requirement of this passage—the unconditional love of God—is reflected clearly in Ps. 73:25-26:

> Whom have I in heaven but thee?
> And there is nothing upon earth that I desire besides thee.
> My flesh and my heart may fail,
> but God is the strength of my heart and my portion for ever.

Rabbinical legend has it that when Abraham and Isaac returned from their ordeal and related to Sarah what had happened, she uttered seven cries and died. Within this same type of contemplation upon the human strain in the narrative, Søren Kierkegaard in *Fear and Trembling* gave four imaginative reconstructions of what might have happened: (1) Abraham unmasked himself as an idolater. The sacrifice was not interrupted. Isaac as he died lost faith in Abraham and claimed God as his father. (2) Abraham carried on as Genesis indicates, with the attested outcome, but he returned to Beersheba angry at God and living the rest of his life without joy. He could never forget what God had required of him, nor forgive God for this harsh requirement. (3) To atone for the sin of wishing to offer Isaac (Abraham's idea, not God's) Abraham went to the altar of Moriah and offered up his own body. (4) The events happened as Genesis records them, but Isaac returned, having lost his faith. Kierkegaard undertook all these reconstructions evidently to show that the story cannot really be explained.

After an extended "Panegyric on Abraham," he then went on to pose three "Problemata": (1) "Is there such a thing as a theological suspension of the ethical?" His answer is "Yes." (2) "Is there such a thing as an absolute duty toward God?" Again his answer is "Yes." There is something a man must do but can never explain. (3) "Was Abraham ethically defensible in keeping silent about his purpose before Sarah, Eliezer, and Isaac?" No one could have understood him. How could he have spoken?

One alternative to the sacrifice of Isaac, that is, giving him up to God, could have been Abraham's worship of Isaac. It is possible to make an idol of the family. This incident shows the relation between members of the family when God is included. The son who is the bridge to the future and the road to fulfillment can be the death of that future, paradoxically not when he is sacrificed to God but when he is cherished unwisely. Here is a father who has to forfeit his son's love and understanding in order to keep him. First love cannot be given to both God and the family anymore than to both God and Mammon. Do we make our families into idols, or do we kneel together as a family before God? Only in that light can we gain courage to deny, discipline, and release them for God's own future.

Perhaps every call to obedience is like Abraham's first call: "By faith Abraham obeyed when he was called to go out to a place which he was to receive as an inheritance; and he went out, not knowing where he was to go" (Heb. 11:8) . The entire paragraph of this chapter is a noble tribute to Abraham's adventurous faith. Match these to a poem by Nancy Byrd Turner bearing the title "When Abraham Went Out of Ur."

> Men go out from the places where they dwelled,
> Knowing not why or whither, but overborne
> At midnight by some awful word foresworn
> Between one dark and day, called and compelled:

So they had gone for ages in the gleam
Of many a daybreak, turning troubled eyes
For one last look at home beneath old skies—
Their birthright bartered for a nameless dream;

Even as God's first adventurer stood forth
One star-wrought night, on a familiar hill,
And saw the Chaldean dawn, remote and chill,
Etching old Ur along the lonely north,
And bowed himself to his loved earth, and rent
His garments, crying he could not go . . . and went.[3]

### Striking Through to Outline

*The first possibility:* The testing of Abraham.

I. Abraham before the test had sacrificed his past to God
II. Abraham in this test is required to sacrifice everything else
    A. His love for his son
    B. His reason for living
    C. Even his religious understanding to God's absurdity
III. Abraham meets the test
IV. God provides for Abraham

*A second possibility:* The testing of Abraham through the sacrifice of Isaac.

I. The son (family)
    A. God's gift
    B. The road to Abraham's future (our reason for living and our road to life's fulfillment)
II. Sacrificing the son (God's requirement over our families)
    A. God's harsh demand (that we love him more than our families)

[3] "When Abraham Went Out of Ur" from *Star in a Well* by Nancy Byrd Turner. Copyright 1935 by Dodd, Mead & Company, Inc. and reprinted by permission of Dodd, Mead & Company, Inc.

    B. The destruction of the future (the expected destruction of our families)

III. God's provision from his own resources

    A. Deliverance for Abraham and Isaac (parents and children are both rescued)

    B. The assurance of the future (the heritage of faith)

*A third possibility:* God's testing in our homes.

  I. Abraham's love of Isaac (we love our families)

    A. Gift of God

    B. The depth of our love

 II. Abraham's love of God (we are highly religious)

    A. God's guiding of Abraham's past

    B. Abraham's past sacrifices for God

III. The conflict of the two loves

    A. The love of God threatens the love of Isaac

        1. God demands the sacrifice of Isaac

        2. God seems to contradict himself

    B. The love of Isaac threatens the love of God

        1. To disobey God to save Isaac would have been to worship Isaac and self instead of God

        2. Such possessive love destroys its object

IV. Abraham's decision: Only one love can remain supreme and that is the love of God

    A. Abraham follows this love to its end, expecting to be destroyed by it

    B. Surprisingly, he finds his fulfillment in it

        1. His vocation

        2. His son restored, not as his own, but as God's gift

*A fourth possibility:* Dying to rise again.

  I. The gift of God: Isaac (the coming of children and our love of families)

II. The claim of God: Abraham required to sacrifice Isaac (first love must nevertheless be given to God, not to families)

III. The crucifixion: The apparent destructiveness of such a claim (everything is lost; a blow at our possessiveness, our security, our self-interest)

IV. The resurrection: Abraham gave his son, but received him back (the family that dies to self-idolatry rises to live a richer life for God)

## The Naming of the Sermon

"Fear and Trembling," Kierkegaard's title for his little book on this narrative might also serve the sermon. "The Testing of Abraham" is so well established as to be inescapable for many. "When Faith Threatens to Destroy the Ground Beneath Us," "Creative Insecurity," "Sacrificing Our Children," and "Undeviating Devotion" are titles that may be used.

# 12

## Preaching on a Major Biblical Theme

Is it possible to preach on a biblical theme? Some would answer with a flat "no," the assumption being that the result is not a sermon but a lecture. That is Karl Barth's answer: "It is not possible, in one sermon, to discourse on a particular subject (thematic preaching) and to expound a passage of Scripture (homiletic)." [1] Since, in Barth's view, a sermon must always expound a passage of scripture, the theme belongs in the lecture hall or in a book of theology; only the exposition of a particular passage of scripture belongs in the pulpit.

Similarly, Jean-Jacques von Allmen in a short homiletical classic warns against the danger of preaching which "proposes themes rather than texts for our preaching, and this thematic treatment of our Sundays, if carried too far, risks making our preaching docetic, perverting our sermons into 'discourses on religious subjects.' Even if the theme is concrete, the very fact that it is a theme gives it an abstract character." [2]

If we accept Barth's stern prohibition against thematic preaching, the subject is closed before we open it. It is logically

[1] *The Preaching of the Gospel,* tr. by B. E. Hooke (Philadelphia: Westminster Press, 1963), p. 58.
[2] *Preaching and Congregation,* p. 39.

194

impossible to go further. For those of von Allmen's persuasion, however, there is a way. It is simply necessary to heed the latter's warning: "When we preach [to people] we are not giving them a lecture; we are intervening in their lives in the name of God to help them, to warn them, to threaten them, to console them, to set them tasks and to give them courage." [3] In other words, a sermon, even when it is on a theme, must be a deed as well as a word; it must enact its truth concretely and in personal terms so as to claim those who hear and him who speaks. In my view, this is a valid insight. It enables us to move forward with the task of this chapter.

## The Need

Meantime, there is an urgent need for the lay understanding of major biblical themes. Central words and phrases of the Bible, such as redemption, justification, grace, kingdom of God, covenant, eternal life, judgment, wrath of God, sin, and death, are nothing but words to millions of confessed, church-going "Christians." Current discussion would indicate that even the word "God" is becoming an empty symbol for many church people.[4]

It is certainly true that the sermon cannot carry the entire educational burden of explaining these themes to a local congregation. There is work that only religious books, classes, and discussion groups can do. Moreover, it is the minister's duty as teacher to see that religious instruction outside the pulpit

[3] *Ibid.*, p. 39.
[4] We are speaking only of church people here. It should not surprise us if nonchurch people find these terms empty; that would help to explain the fact that they are outsiders. But if insiders continue to find them empty, it is only a matter of time until they will join the outsiders in their unbelief. The task of making biblical doctrines live, therefore, is not an academic matter. It is an evangelical concern of first importance.

goes forward with great energy and through every efficient means at his command. In this educational task, the minister is not simply an executive, though he is that also; he is chief teacher, and he should be spending large blocks of time in teaching actual classes, groups, and individuals.[5]

When all this is said, however, the fact remains that the Sunday morning congregation is the largest possible audience that a minister now has, that it is several times as large as any instructional group he can presently assemble. Is there any reason why he should meet them week after week but leave them ignorant of doctrinal meanings? Is a sermon so "inspirational," or "kerygmatic," or "hortatory," that the people have no right to know what inspires them, what is proclaimed, or what they are exhorted to do and believe? The fact is that the absence of sound teaching makes everything else vacant. The didactic and kerygmatic sides of the gospel cannot be separated, one to be assigned to the pulpit, the other to the church school. When approached primarily as education—as in the church school—the gospel must address us in a kerygmatic framework. And when approached primarily as proclamation—as from the pulpit—the gospel must speak to us in its didactic framework. To separate one from the other is to kill both.

Though much of this instructional responsibility within sermons may be discharged in short paragraphs, sentences, or even in synonyms (like identifying the names of persons figuring in a newspaper story) these pieces of doctrinal instruction need to be unified in an occasional sermon devoted entirely to one doctrine. Such sermons give perspective; they provide theo-

---

[5] In the scheduling of these classes, there is no law which says that they have to be at 10 A.M. on Sunday morning. The time of instruction is not a part of the commandment; the task of instruction is.

logical horizons, so essential in orienting listeners to particular texts.

The purpose of such doctrinal sermons is not definition, which is often the translation of one abstraction into another, but pointing toward and participating in the concrete realities out of which the name of the doctrine arose. It is the transfiguration of a word into an experienced meeting between the hearer and the action of God. Sometimes this requires nothing more than getting the name and the reality together—the hearer has been experiencing the reality under discussion for years, but he has never known its biblical name or has not identified it in that way. Sometimes it involves pointing beyond the hearer's present level of religious experience to a momentous possibility for his future development. This is more difficult. But in neither case is a doctrine merely an impersonal idea; it is a fact about God's action as a person experiences or may experience it.

How is a man to proceed in growing such a sermon?

## Ways of Preparing

(1) *Select a key word or phrase from the Bible.* One good way of doing this is to take one of the more theological letters of the New Testament, such as Colossians, Romans, Galatians, or Ephesians, and go through it underscoring all the theological terms. Lift these out on a separate piece of paper; eliminate duplications or make logical combinations; then select the major ones and set them in order for future treatment in the pulpit. This method of selection has the virtue of rising out of particular passages of scripture and so may rise above the danger of flying away into philosophical abstractions. Further, by making the language of theological discussion biblical, the sermon will both enrich the liturgical reading of scripture and

be enriched by it. Emotional and intellectual meanings will strengthen and reinforce each other.

There are a number of good books on biblical key words.[6] Selection of doctrines for the pulpit may, of course, be made directly from one of them. Or the theme may arise from pastoral conversations in which certain questions point up instructional needs. A card file or commonplace book of such conversations not only gives a theme but places it in a life situation, with which the sermon may often begin.

(2) *Study the biblical key word selected, using the best word-books and biblical dictionaries available.* (See footnote 6 for the best of these.) Such study should be comprehensive, covering the treatment of the doctrine through the whole biblical record. It will be more helpful than a concordance in pointing to important biblical texts.

(3) *From among the many passages of scripture embodying a doctrine, select the more significant texts, both long and short.* List them. It may be that you will finally choose a single text

---

[6] Leader of all wordbooks is Gerhard Kittel's multi-volume *Theologisches Wörterbuch zum Neuen Testament* requiring a knowledge of both Greek and German. This is now being translated into English by William B. Eerdman's Publishing Company of Grand Rapids, Michigan; three volumes are now ready and others will follow in series. Both Harper & Row (3 vols.) and Adams and Charles Black of London (14 vols.) have published a limited number of these key words in English translation. Alan Richardson's *A Theological Word Book of the Bible* (New York: Macmillan, 1951), though far briefer than Kittel, covers the most important theological terms, as does J. J. von Allmen's *A Companion to the Bible* (New York: Oxford University Press, 1958). William Barclay's two books, *New Testament Wordbook* (1955) and *More New Testament Words* (1958) by Alec P. Allenson, Naperville, Ill. and Harper & Row, New York, respectively are based on Greek but are so engagingly written as to be especially inviting to anyone with homiletical interests. Older works of proven value include Richard C. Trench's *Synonyms of the New Testament* (9th ed.; London: Macmillan, 1880); Marvin R. Vincent's *Word Studies in the New Testament,* (4 vols.; New York: Charles Scribner's Sons, 1887-1900); and Burton's *New Testament Word Studies* (Chicago: University of Chicago Press, 1927).

for the sermon or a series of texts for the developing stages of movement within the sermon. In any case, the anomaly of a sermon on a biblical theme which does not quote or use any passage of scripture will be obvious. This anomaly should be avoided.

(4) *Check your study of the scriptures against your own personal knowledge of the doctrine by personal encounter.* We are here talking about what the semanticists call "extensional meanings" (concrete, life situation meanings) as opposed to "intentional meanings" (dictionary definitions or mere conceptualizations spun off in words). Can you point to the reality of the doctrine in your own vital experience? For example, if the topic is *forgiveness,* the questions may well be: "Have I ever experienced God's forgiveness? For what? When and where? Through what person? With what results? How do I know that I am forgiven?" This is pointing; it is seeking for extensional meanings. It is knowledge by experience rather than by reason alone—what the Germans call *kennenlernen* as opposed to *wissen.* Planning a sermon about a doctrine for which there is no resource of personal experience is like trying to erect a building by starting with the fourth floor. It can be nothing but an air castle. There are doctrines that are not as yet real, even to seminary graduates and experienced pastors. We have to grow into them. Until we do we cannot really preach on them; we will merely lecture about them.

(5) *Now enlarge the extensional meaning of the theme by locating its operation in the lives of people you know, including those in your own parish.* In a word, having studied your Bible and yourself for the theme, now study your congregation. Of the resultant sermon, a hearer should not say, "He is talking about such-and-such a doctrine this morning." Rather, he should say, "Why, he's talking about me!" The best theological

preaching does not so label itself; its motivation is fundamentally pastoral.

## Toward a Sermon with Deductive Structure

If you want to proceed in the traditional way, by beginning with a text which you then expound, the steps to be followed from this point forward are fairly obvious. It is the pattern outlined in the chapters of Part II in this book. You will choose a single passage or a chain of passages (not too many!) to bear the sermon. You will set the text or texts in context, exegete them, relate yourself to them, write the aim and proposition of the passage or passages, and go on to develop the sermon in the accustomed manner.

The disadvantage of this type of outline for theological preaching is that the hearers must begin with a term or terms which may be largely void of meaning. Unless the sermon moves quickly to connect the term to their experience, they may be unable to listen with any sense of personal involvement. They confront the text before they are ready for it, before they find themselves involved in its truth. Suspecting the minister of preaching about an abstract idea rather than about them, they may switch him off almost before he begins.

When the traditional, deductive structure is decided upon, the preacher may begin with the text, but in the very next sentence he must get to the hearer. Better still, in most cases the sermon should begin with the hearer, then move as quickly as possible to the hearer's personal stake in the text. When the theme is fairly "cold" or evidently remote from the everyday language of laymen, it may be difficult to involve the hearer at once. He may need more preparation. In that case, it may be wiser to invert the relationship of text to sermon—that is, to end with the text rather than begin with it. This brings us to our next topic and to a different kind of sermon structure.

## Toward a Sermon with Inductive Structure

A doctrinal sermon may advantageously end with the text, rather than begin with it. This is not to say that the sermon in preparation rises outside the scripture. In conception, this sermon begins with the text no less than the traditional sermon does. It differs from the traditional pattern only in execution.

Let me illustrate from the nomination of a candidate for political office at a convention of his party. The nominator usually withholds the nominee's name until the end of his speech. He knows the man's name, has him in mind from the beginning, prepares the speech for the sole purpose of putting that man in nomination. But he wants to bring out the full significance of the name before he pronounces it. He wants the name of his nominee to be the climax of his speech. In conceiving the speech, the name came first; in delivering it the name comes last.

A good inductive sermon is like an effective nominating speech. It develops the full significance of the text before pronouncing it; then at the climax of the sermon it unveils the text in all its splendor. By this time the text, which might have been like an empty, echoing chamber if it had been spoken at the beginning without adequate preparation, now welcomes the hearer like the hearth fire of an inviting living room. This sermon is not less expository than the other; it merely uses a different method of exposition, one suited especially to the exploration of unoccupied territory or the discovery of new truth.

Let us take an example of such a sermon from James A. Pike's book *A New Look in Preaching*.[7] This is a sermon on

[7] (New York: Charles Scribner's Sons, 1961), pp. 38-46.

"justification by grace through faith unto good works," a highly doctrinal subject which is also completely biblical. Bishop Pike approaches this sermon through depth psychology, an approach for which our whole culture prepares us, one congenial to our age. He develops it by way of simple analogy, reserving the text itself until the sermon has made its point.

I. *The problem: the reconciliation of self-criticism with self-acceptance.*

How can one be really honest with oneself, avoiding rationalizations —and still live with oneself? A man needs self-acceptance or he can't live with himself; he needs self-criticism or others can't live with him. The two sound irreconcilable. People tend to think they can't have both; so they choose self-acceptance. And they achieve this by a process of rationalization and excuse-making.

II. *An analysis of the process of rationalization.* This analysis begins with a few quick examples of rationalization: "Anything to make us feel all right with ourselves." Then the analysis moves on to assay the results of such cover-ups: (1) They numb the sense of self-criticism—and keep a person from growing as a human being from what he is toward what he ought to be. (2) They do not obliterate our sense of guilt; these rationalizations "simply put blankets on top of it and cause it to sink down into the subconscious where it makes us sick." This connection between guilt and psychosomatic sickness is discussed: "Obviously this does not mean that everyone you know who is sick is therefore guilty. But it does mean that a man who is guilty and doesn't know how to handle it will be sick. You can be sure of that. He will be sick."

III. *A restatement of the problem, which has now become more urgent:* "How do you avoid shoving a sense of guilt down into the unconscious, and how do you avoid carrying it around in the conscious mind?"

IV. *The solution given in analogy:* a story about the handling of garbage in a summer cabin on Cape Cod. Let us use Bishop Pike's own words:

We were moving into our summer house on Cape Cod about ten summers ago. We started out from New York in plenty of time to stock in all the food needed for the next day. But due to too many stops for four children for too many purposes we were late in getting there. But we did finally find a light in a little "general store" and succeeded in making purchases of what we needed for breakfast. I did have the wisdom to buy one of those three-cornered things for the kitchen sink. Well, by mid-morning that was full; and as I was going downtown to stock in anyway, I told my wife that I would buy a more adequate receptacle: I bought a step-on can. That was full by the next morning, and she then said, "Jim, you've got to get at this problem more basically"; so I took the back seat out of the station wagon and went into a hardware store in a larger town nearby and got a great big galvanized can—in fact two of them. That solved the problem for a week. Then what? You know how these modern houses are today—lots of closet space.

Here the congregation gets the point—and it's time to move back to the analogue, by some such statement as, "nor is it healthy to suppress guilt in the subconscious." But one shouldn't move on quite yet to the Gospel answer: the people are still wondering what happened in the analogy. Hence, after a pause: "You're probably wondering what we decided to do [they were]; well, we decided to arrange for an outside agency to take it off our hands."

Now, you see the congregation ready for the Gospel. Right now is the time to affirm that the unique thing about the Christian faith is that we believe in a God who has the resources to take all the sin, all the hurt, yes all the filth of the world unto Himself. This is our central teaching. This is why in our iconography the central feature is the Cross—not the Golden Rule, not the Summary of the

203

Law. I said once in a sermon that as to the moral universe God is the great Garbage Collector; and I offended a nice old lady who gave the Church $1,000 a year. I don't say that anymore. But I meant to say it: He is, you know.[8]

The point is, in summary, you can't keep it around the conscious mind (the "kitchen" you simply *must* tidy up once in a while), and you don't dare lock it up in a closet. Who's to take it away? The "Lamb of God who takest away the sins of the world." God meets us where we are, not where we ought to be, takes the hurt out of our lives, accepts us even though we are not acceptable. . . .

The preacher can develop this further; for example, to avoid the "free ride" feeling ("Should we sin the more that grace abound?") He can indicate that the Christian is a man who accepts himself, though unacceptable, because God accepts him, and *therefore* in grateful response to that gift is an expert in taking up the hurts in the lives of other people. . . .

V. *The solution given in the language of the text.* In Bishop Pike's words:

Now is the time to give the copyright notice. There are preachers in our Church who are very good at explaining things in plain terms where people live, but who never mention any traditional names. . . . Therefore, I always say at the end of a sermon—take for example this one: "Now this is what the Church has always meant by *justification* (which doesn't mean being right, it means being taken for right) *by grace* (not earned, sheer gift) *through faith* (responding

[8] Lest it appear that the forgiveness of sin is as easy as getting the sanitation department to call for the garbage, the preacher needs to make it clear that the struggle to receive forgiveness is one "in fear and trembling," even in agony unto death. Intellectualization of personal processes must not be allowed to substitute for the costly surrender of mind and heart and will, which is usually possible only after passing through the dark valley of intense emotional resistance. Certainly the sermon cannot achieve this as an act of fiat for its listeners. The best it can do is to open minds and hearts to its possibility and to prompt the searching dialogue in which the event of deliverance can begin to take place.

in repentance and in belief in the promises of a God who is everlastingly this way, whose very nature and property is to forgive and have mercy) *unto good works,* good works as the fruits of the free gift of salvation—not as the wages of salvation . . .

The labels come in very well if people have understood up to this point that you have been talking about *them.* Now you can talk the language of traditional theology: justification, and sanctification as the fruit of justification.

Though Bishop Pike did not go on to tie the doctrine to specific biblical texts, he might well have done so. Then his sermon, inverting the customary order, would have ended with his text, having brought his hearers to the point where biblical insight might dawn upon them.

## A Second Case Study

Take another example, this time a sermon of my own on the text, "By grace you have been saved through faith; and this is not your own doing, it is the gift of God" (Eph. 2:8). As in the preceding example, the text will be reserved until we are prepared for it, toward the end of the sermon. But unlike the previous sermon, we will gradually build up toward it, forecasting the biblical language through echoing phrases which sound at intervals through the sermon, the phrases being: "not your own doing" and "the gift of God."

The sermon is called "Reaping More Than We Sow." It is designed to overcome our egocentric resistance to the simple fact that we are all the time receiving far more than we can earn or deserve in all areas of life, the moral realm included. Its method is not analogy but example—example upon example, registering its point by bombardment:

"In the year 1940 Perry Hayden, a farmer living near Tecumseh, Michigan, went to church one Sunday and heard his pastor preach a sermon on a text from John 12:24, 'Except a

205

corn of wheat fall into the ground and die, it abideth alone: but if it die, it bringeth forth much fruit' (KJV). Farmer Hayden did not forget his sermon, but kept turning it over in his mind until it grew into a project. He took a tiny measure, one cubic inch in volume, and filled it with wheat. By actual count it held 360 grains. These kernels Hayden planted in a plot of ground four feet wide by eight feet long. At the following harvest he reaped the grain, threshed it, and after withholding a tenth for his church replanted the rest. It seeded a plot of ground twenty-four by sixty feet, and the harvest from that plot, minus the tithe, was sufficient to plant one acre. Hayden kept on with his experiment for five years. By the third year his original measure of 360 grains had multiplied until it had planted fourteen acres. The fourth year this moved up to 250 acres; and the fifth year it required 2,000 acres. This dramatic demonstration of nature's laws of increase caught the imagination of the world. It was captured in motion picture film and by the pages of *Life* magazine.

"Perry Hayden was a religious man. He knew that man can plant and cultivate but that it is God who gives the increase: pressed down, shaken together, and running over. Concerning his own part in the demonstration, he could have said: *It was not my own doing; it was the gift of God.*"

Next I tell of a summer garden inundated by the flooding of bottom land in the bend of a creek. Out of twenty-four broccoli plants, only six survived. "Those six remaining plants produced all the broccoli our family of four could eat that summer and enough for several of the neighbors. Such is the law of harvest—thirtyfold, sixtyfold and a hundredfold. Not only do we reap what we sow, but more than we sow, and *it is not our own doing; it is the gift of God.*"

The third example was taken from the fracturing, setting, and mending of my son's leg bone when he was a small boy:

"In due time the bone was set, placed in a cast and the tissues began to mend. The doctor said, 'Now we have to wait on nature.' If he had cared to say it in biblical language, he could have said: *The mending of bones is not my doing; it is the gift of God.*"

A fourth example is from the world of culture and education. The multiplication table, the alphabet, the art of writing, and a great treasury of knowledge are ours for the asking plus a small investment of study. Suppose we had to invent the alphabet and the art of writing and printing! "It could be stated in biblical language: Education *is not our own doing;* through our social inheritance *it is the gift of God.*"

We move on to yet a fifth example; this lesson has to be driven home line upon line. "What one of us did not receive the love of parents and friends when we were tiny? While we were yet helpless babes and before we had proved that we could be worth our salt we were nursed, clothed, sheltered, and loved. There is no strutting man pounding his chest and proclaiming that he is self-made who did not begin his life and continue through many dependent years, receiving what he had not sown, out of the superabundance of the love of God expressed through his family. Of these infant and childhood years we all could say: *It was not our own doing; it was the gift of God.*"

"The emerging principle—the amplitude of God's free gifts, far beyond the measure of our deserving—can be seen in growth of crops, in the transmission of our cultural heritage, and in the healing of wounds and mending of broken bones. What about the deeper wounding, the inner brokenness that we suffer when we fail to do what we want, and even do what we hate? It is not so much that we break a moral law as that we are breaking the law of our own being. Is there any healing for that?

"Let us illustrate. Here is a man driving down a city street; he grows careless and inattentive at the wheel. As a result he runs over a four-year-old child, the only son of a widowed mother. The courts find him guilty of manslaughter and send him to prison for a year. When he comes out, there may be some who will say, 'He has paid for his crime. He is all square with the law.' But if he is a sensitive man—that is to say, if he is fully human—he will know that he has not paid for his crime and that he can never pay for it. He has not merely broken the law. He has broken a mother's heart. Now suppose he tries to mend that broken heart with money, large sums of money—not so much to make up for what he has taken from her as to be at peace with himself. That will not work either. There is no way to find peace, in fact, save one. That is if the bereaved mother will forgive him. If she will absorb the loss, become a woman of sorrows and acquainted with grief, yet with compassion and understanding for his sorrow, she can forgive him. Then and then alone will that man be at peace with himself. But it will be a sober peace. Never again will you find him driving recklessly down a residential street.

"Do you see what I am saying? Your sin. It is not the breaking of a few laws that you can pay for by a few penitential prayers and a few works of charity. You do not sin against God's law. You sin against his love. Is there anyone who is not guilty of resenting or hating another human being? Perhaps you do not want to put it that strongly. Annoyed, irritated, resentful—yes; but hostile or hating—no. Well, of course, irritation, resentment, hostility—all are milder or stronger forms of the same thing. Mild or intense, they are all hatred. John puts the enormity of that crime bluntly: 'Any one who hates his brother is a murderer' (I John 3:15). Anyone who despises another human being is guilty, not of manslaughter, but of murder. Carry the crime even deeper; see it as it really is.

208

'Inasmuch as ye have done it unto one of the least of these my brethren, ye have done it unto me,' Jesus said (KJV). It is not merely that you have murdered your brother; you have struck an assassin's blow at God himself.

"This is what sin is ultimately—the attempt to assassinate God and to usurp his throne. To kill God so we can be our own gods. The enormity of our crime is silhouetted in dark outline against the flaming sky. Moreover, all would be hopeless were it not for the fact that God absorbs the blow. For, we say, if I am such an assassin, why am I free? Why am I not behind bars; or why have I not been hanged by the neck until dead?

"There is only one answer: Except for God's astounding generosity all would be dead. Put it in the language of Ephesians: 'But God, who is rich in mercy, out of the great love with which he loved us, even when we were dead through our trespasses, made us alive together with Christ. . . . For by grace you have been saved through faith; and this is not your own doing, it is the gift of God.'

"How slow we are to see this. How deluded by the opposite view, how resentful that we do not get what we think we deserve. Let us thank God that we do not get what we deserve, for as Portia said to Shylock in the *Merchant of Venice,* 'Though justice be thy plea . . . none of us should see salvation.' Thank God, we get more than we deserve. Attwater in Robert Louis Stevenson's *Ebb-Tide* said it: 'Why not the grace of your Maker and Redeemer, He who died for you, He who upholds you, He whom you daily crucify afresh? There is nothing but God's grace. We walk upon it, we breathe it; we live and die by it; it makes the nails and axles of the universe.' "

Preaching on a major biblical theme need not be abstract lecture. It should always be biblical. It can usually be textual. But instead of taking the text as the point of departure, why not make it the port of arrival?

# Epilogue
## Servant of the Word

Much more could be said. We could linger in the laboratory to work with legal literature, folk songs, folk sagas, short stories, speeches, prayers, court records, allegories, letters, and essays. Anyone who has come this far, however, will know that types of biblical literature not yet studied tend to impose their own criteria. A battle cry cannot be interpreted in the same way as a commandment, nor a folk saga as a court record. Once this principle is established, it will be a simple matter to discover in each case the ruling principles which will allow each type of literature to speak in its own medium and by its own native power.

The search for principles and rules of interpretation and ways of working which has engaged our attention is not a quest for a secret formula which will unlock the closed box of scripture. It is rather an effort to clear away the obstructions which prevent us from hearing the clear Word which already sounds through the Scriptures. We are not biblical mechanics, spiritual locksmiths. We are men whom God has called into being by his creative Word. We are children of God whom he has raised from sin and death by his redemptive Word. And we are mes-

sengers whom he has commissioned by his reconciling Word. In short, we are servants of the Word.

A true servant has a work to perform. He submits to discipline, follows a regimen. It does not have to be the one suggested in this book, but surely it cannot be less demanding. The nineteenth-century religious reformer Alexander Campbell had a fine phrase in which he characterized the attitude of one who takes the Bible seriously. Thinking of a speaker addressing a concourse of people in a grove, and bearing in mind a man on the fringe of the crowd, he pointed out that there was such a thing as "the understanding distance." If a man stood beyond the range of the speaker's voice, it was not the speaker's fault if he did not hear. The understanding distance within which one must stand to hear God speak through the Bible cannot be measured in feet and yards, to be sure, but it does have some delimiting characteristics, one of which is willingness to read and study. The slothful proclaimer of the Word simply refuses to put himself within the range.

There is more. To come within the understanding distance a servant of the Word comes to the living Word, that is, to God himself. Translate the noun, Word, into a verb, and the implication is at once apparent: The Word of God is God himself *speaking*. The proclaimer of the Word, therefore, begins as a man who is himself being addressed—called into being, wounded, and healed by the living God. The degree of a man's service to the Word of God will depend in no small part upon the depth of his personal relationship to God. His human words will have power to the extent that they originate in God's speaking personally to him and in his own listening response. This is a daily renewal, for the verb is not in the past tense; the God who speaks is speaking today. Thus a true servant of the Word is something more than a hard worker.

There is still another aspect of the understanding distance.

This is the service of God where he is—in the midst of his people. An ambassador of reconciliation must himself be reconciled; he must be a member of the covenant people. When he speaks to these people, he also speaks as one of them. If he speaks against them, as sometimes he must, he also speaks for them. At this point all the gains of life situation preaching become available to him. Life situation sermons and biblical sermons need not—indeed, they cannot—exclude each other. Every genuine sermon is a part of the dialogue of worship between God and people. These people are men of their own time, with their own unique apprehensions of the human predicament. To speak for God is to speak to them in concrete terms with a high degree of communicative relevance. Never, not in a single paragraph of a sermon, should a minister lose sight of those to whom he speaks. Preaching is a function of the pastoral office.

The rewards of such servanthood are immense. A minister—and "minister" means "servant"—may enter into this role fearfully, expecting that by placing his pulpit ministry under the discipline of scripture he will be consenting to a kind of narrow bondage. What he will discover is quite different: Instead of a narrow world, he will enter into one immeasurably wider, deeper, and higher; his invention and creativity, far from being stunted, will grow amazingly. Instead of limitation and bondage, he will discover new freedom. By submerging his own personal authority to that of scripture, he may expect to lose stature, only to find that he is now speaking with unaccustomed authority and power. There are great satisfactions in biblical preaching for the man who stands up to preach.

Beyond the satisfactions of the preacher, however, are the far more important results in the congregation. Suddenly people who have been receiving stones—perhaps even the polished gems of our human wisdom—will look up and be fed loaves of bread. The fog of biblical illiteracy will begin gradually to lift and to be wafted away on a fresh breeze of insight and Christian joy. The horizontal dreariness of life, "drifting to and fro on the misty flats," will be pierced from above by the vertical rays of a divine illumination, and the commonplace will be lifted and exalted into significance.

As I bring this work to a close, I do so with the firm conviction that a new epoch of pulpit power lies ahead for the man who will give up his dream of being a master of assemblies and learn, painfully and slowly, how to become a genuine servant of the Word.

# Index of Scripture

## Old Testament

**Genesis**
1:2 .......................... 78
1:9, 11 ...................... 34
12:1-3 .......................182
15:3-5 .......................182
16:1-16 ......................183
18:9-15 ......................183
21:1-8 .......................183
21:9-21 ......................183
22:1-19 ...................181-93
25:21-34; 27-35; 37-50 ......94-106
25:26; 27:36 ................. 96
25:32-33 ..................... 96
27:27 ........................ 96
28:19 ........................ 96
30:14 ........................ 97
30:37 ........................ 97
31:19, 30, 32, 33-35 ............ 97
31:49 ........................ 97
32:27-29 ..................... 97
32:30-31 ..................... 98
48:15 ........................101

**Exodus**
3:20 .........................127*n*
4:8 ..........................127*n*
4:24-26 ......................179
7:9 ..........................127*n*
13:1-2 .......................184

**Exodus—cont'd**
13:3 ......................... 26
13:11-16 .....................184
33:20, 23 ..................103-4
34:20 ........................ 26

**Leviticus**
18:21 ........................184
20:2 .........................183

**Numbers**
3:11-13, 40-51 ...............184
18:15-16 .....................184
18:15-18 ..................... 26

**Deuteronomy**
12:30-31 .....................183
13:3 .........................185

**Joshua**
6 ............................180
7 ..........................178-79

**Judges**
2:22 .........................185
11 ........................... 20
11:29-40 .....................178
19 ...........................179
21:25 ........................103

**I Samuel**
15 ........................179-80

**II Samuel**
12:1-6 ......................108

**II Kings**
3:27 ......................184
4:42-44 ...................135
16:3, 17, 31 ..............183
23:10 ..............183, 184

**Job**
1:6-12 ....................185

**Psalms**
19:2-4 .................... 34
22:1-2 ....................161
33:6 ...................... 38
39:2-3 .................... 77
39:3 ...................... 78
41:4 ...................... 30
46:10 .............148-49, 156
73:25-26 ..................189
106:37-38 .................183
130:1-3 ...................161
130:7-8 ................... 27
139 ...................164-77

**Isaiah**
1:18 ...................... 29
6:10 ...................... 30
9:2-7 ..................... 29
11:1-9 .................... 29
27:18-19 .................. 30
55:10-11 ..................122
65:17 ..................... 29

**Jeremiah**
1:4 ...................... 38
6:16 ......................170
7:30-32 ...................183
8:22 ...................... 30
17:10 .....................165
17:14 ..................... 30
19:3-5 ....................183
30:17 ..................... 30
32:35 .....................184
36 ....................... 38

**Ezekiel**
16:20-21 ..................183

**Hosea**
6:1 ...................... 30
12:2-6 ....................103

**Micah**
6:7 ......................184

### New Testament

**Matthew**
5:24 ..................... 31n
7:21-23 ................... 15
12:38-39 .................128n
14:13a-21a ...............131
15:32-39 .................131
16:1-4 ...................128n
21:18-19 .................130
22:1-14 ..................136
24:1–25:46 ...............115
25:14-30 ..............115-25

**Mark**
6:30-44 ..................131
8:1-10 ...................131
8:11-12 ..................128n
9:39 .....................128n
10:45 ..................... 27
11:12-14, 20-25 ..........130

**Luke**
5:31-32 ................... 30
9:10-17 ..................131
11:16 ....................128n
11:52 ....................117
13:6-9 ...................130
14:16-24 .................136
23:8 .....................128

**John**
1:14 ...................... 38
3:3, 6-7 .................. 29
3:6 ......................147
6:1-13 ...................131
6:4 ......................133
17:3 .....................155

**Acts**
2:22 .....................128n

## Romans

1:19-20 ....................... 38
2:12-16 ...................... 38
3:22-25a ..................... 28
5:10, 11 ..................... 31n
6:1-11 ....................... 29
6:1-14 .......................104
6:4 .......................... 29
8:2 .......................... 26
8:24 .........................147
11:15 ........................ 31n

## I Corinthians

2:6 .......................... 32n
3:11 ......................... 32
5:7 .......................... 28
7:14 ......................... 20
9:17 .........................118
12 ........................... 64
13 ........................... 64
14 ........................... 64
14:20 ........................ 32n
15:19 ........................155

## II Corinthians

2:16 .........................140
5:1 ..........................155
5:17 ......................... 29
5:18-20 ...................... 31n
6:14 ......................... 20

## Galatians

2:7 ..........................118

## Ephesians

1:7 .......................... 28
1:13 .........................154
2:8 ..........................205
2:16 ......................... 31n
4:13 ......................... 32n

## Philippians

3:15 ......................... 32n
4:13 .........................138

## Colossians

1:15 .........................154
1:17 ......................... 85
1:20 ......................... 31n
1:28 ......................... 32n
3:21-23 ...................... 84
4:12 ......................... 32n

## I Timothy

6:20 .........................118

## II Timothy

1:8 ..........................154
1:13, 14 .....................154
2:3 ..........................154
2:15 .........................154

## Titus

1:3 ..........................118

## Hebrews

4:12-13 ...................... 15
9:12 ......................... 28
9:22 ......................... 28
11:8 .........................190
11:12 ........................183

## James

2:19 ......................... 23
4:1-10 .......................103

## II Peter

3:4 ..........................116

## I John

1:7 .......................... 28
3:15 .........................208
4:20 .........................147
5:4 ..........................140

## Revelation

5:9 .......................... 28
21 ........................... 29

# Index of Names and Subjects

Abraham, 33, 181-93
accidental occasion, 80, 84
Achan's sin, 178, 181
*Act of Creation, The* (Koestler), 83
Agag, King of Amalek, 49, 179
Alcoholics Anonymous, 123
Alpha and Omega, 143
alterant, 152
analogy, 26-33, 108-10
*Apostolic Preaching and Its Development, The* (Dodd), 59
assassinating God, 209
authoritarianism, 158

*Bald Soprano, The* (Ionesco), 85
ban, the (devoted thing), 179, 180
Barclay, William, 134, 135
*Barriers to Christian Belief* (Griffith), 129
Barth, Karl, 37, 59, 194
Bethel, 96-97
Bible
chapter and verse division, 146
correct reading of: concepts in conflict, 49-50; cultural translation, 54; as men's words, 49; mirroring modern men, 55; nonrevelatory approaches, 52; peaks and valleys, 49-50; probing the reader, 50-52; reading in faith, 50; types of literature, 53, 211

Bible—*cont'd*
key words, 197-99: books on, 198*n*
misreading: as answering curiosity, 20-21; as cultural treasury, 25; as dogma, 23-24; as fetish, 23; as human quest, 24; as law, 18-20; misplaced offense, 54; as predictive, 20-21; as science, 21-23
purpose of, 17-19: as catalytic agent, 44, 48-49; as containing contemporary man, 47-48, 50; inadequate answers, 19-24; as record of past meetings of God and men, 47; as revelation-redemption, 24-25
*Bible in the Nineteenth Century, The* (Carpenter), 17
biblical preaching
creative preparation, 75-87
distinguished from quoting, 71-72
more than lecture, 75
never antiquarian, 72-73
selective, 73-74
bibliolatry, 38
bisociation, 83
Blackman, Edwin Cyril, 17
blood atonement (propitiation, expiation, sacrifice), 27-29
brainstorming, 79
on feeding of five thousand, 138-44
on Jacob, 102-4

brainstorming—*cont'd*
 on parable of talents, 121-23
 on psalm 139, 174-76,
 on testing of Abraham, 189-91
Bread of Life, 133
brooding: *see* brainstorming
Brunner, Emil, 31, 44
Buber, Martin, 31
Bultmann, Rudolf, 31, 50, 67
Bunyan, Paul, 178
Burgon, John, 17

Cadoux, A. T., 111
Caesarea Philippi, Peter's Confession,
 132
Caiaphas, 128-29
Calvin, John, 39
Campbell, Alexander, 37-38, 212
Carpenter, J. Estlin, 17
catacombs, Roman, 136
*Christian System, The* (Campbell), 38
Christian year, 147, 153
circumcision, 179, 181
*Companion to the Bible, A,* 128
conscience, 51
covenant, 185
covenant community, 43
creative homiletics, 75-87
creative Word, 39, 41

David, King of Israel, 108-10
death of God theology, 175
dialogue, 68
didactic preaching, 196
Diehl, Charles F., 81
*Divine-Human Encounter* (Brunner),
 44
doctrinal sermons, 194-209
 danger of abstraction, 197
 deductive structure, 200
 example from James A. Pike, 201-5
 inductive structure, 201-9
 need for, 195-97
 "Reaping More Than We Sow,"
 205-9
 ways of preparing, 197-200
Dodd, C. H., 59

*Ebb-Tide* (Stevenson), 209
Ebeling, Gerhard, 36, 51-52
Egyptian bondage, 43
eisegesis, 154
elder brother, 14, 15
Eliezer of Damascus, 182
Elisha, 135
entrusted word, 117
estrangement, 81, 103
eternal life, 155
*Eternal Now, The* (Tillich), 48
Étienne, Robert, 146, 148
et-Tabgha, 136
Eucharist: *see* Lord's Supper
ewe lamb, parable of, 108-10
exegesis
 of feeding of five thousand, 133-36
 of Jacob, 96-98
 of parable of talents, 117-19
 of psalm 139, 165-70
 of testing of Abraham, 184-86
expository preaching, 61, 146

family idolatry, 190
*Fear and Trembling* (Kierkegaard),
 189, 193
feeding of the five thousand, 131-45
Fosdick, Harry Emerson, 130-31
free association, 79
frustration, 78

Galileo, 22, 80
Gandhi, Mahatma, 140
Garrison, W. E., 143
Geneva Convention, 179, 180
genocide, crime of, 179
*Gleichzeitigkeit,* 120
Glueck, Nelson, 104
gnosticism, 42
God
 assassination of, 209
 death of, 175
 as Great Garbage Collector, 204
 in history, 42-45
 knowledge of, 157, 175
 who hides himself, 175
Gospel of the Nazarenes, 114

grace, 204-9
Great Physician, 30
Griffith, A. Leonard, 128-29
growing into maturity, 32
guilt, 202-5

habit, 86-87
Hagar, 182-83
*Harper's Bible Dictionary*, 94
Haselden, Kyle, 150-52
*Hastings' Dictionary of the Bible*, 94
Hayden, Perry, 206
healing, 30-31
heaven, 25
hermeneutics: *see* interpretation
Herod Antipas, 132, 142
Hitler, Adolf, 179
Hobbes, Thomas, 102-3
Holy Spirit, 48, 85
homiletics, 71-87
  creative approach, 75-87
  false approaches, 71-75
Horney, Karen, 102
*How to Think Creatively* (Hutchinson), 76
Howe, John, 147
human sacrifice, 20, 178, 179, 181, 183-84
Hunter, A. M., 111
Hutchinson, Eliot D., 76

imagination, 86
incubation, 77, 79
Index of Prohibited Books, 22
insight, 76, 77, 79-80, 83
*In the Minister's Workshop* (Luccock), 14
*Integrity of Preaching, The* (Knox), 150
interpretation of the Bible, 16, 17
  biographies, 92-94
  legend or myth, 178-81
  miracles, 127-31
  parables, 107-14
  presuppositions, 46-57
  psalms, 159-64
  steps in, 58-70
  theme (doctrine), 197-200

*Interpreter's Dictionary of the Bible, The*, 94
"Interrelation of Phases in the Process of Insight," diagram, 76
Ionesco, Eugene, 85
Irenaeus, 111
Isaac, 181, 182, 183, 185, 187, 190

Jabbok River, 101
Jacob, 92-106
  at Bethel, 96-97
  birthright, 96
  blessing, 96
  context of life, 95-96
  episodes of life, 94-95
  name, 96, 97
  at Penuel, 98, 103, 104
Jacob, sermon on
  aim, 99
  brainstorming, 102-4
  dynamics, 100
  names, 106
  outlines, 104-6
  précis, 100-101
  proposition, 99-100
Jephtha's vow, 20, 178
Jeremiah, 57
Jeremias, Joachim, 112, 115, 116, 117
Jericho, 178-79, 180
*Jesus Christ and Mythology* (Bultmann), 50
Jews, murder of, 179
John the Baptist, 132
*John Calvin, Expository Preacher* (Nixon), 39
Johnson, James Weldon, 35
judgment, 55
Jülicher, Adolph, 111
justification by faith, 201-5

kerygmatic preaching, 196
Kierkegaard, Søren, 189, 193
knowledge of God, 157, 175
Knox, John, 73, 150
Koestler, Arthur, 83

Laban, 97, 101
Langston, Archbishop Stephen, 146

Lanier, Sidney, 175
Leah, 101
legalism, 18, 19, 20, 21
legend: *see* perplexing passage
Levite's concubine, 179
life situation preaching, 213
Locke, John, 37
Lord's Prayer, in outline, 74
Lord's Supper, 136, 140, 141
Luccock, Halford E., 14
Luther, Martin, 39-40, 159

manna, 136
major biblical theme: *see* doctrinal
    sermons
messianic banquet, 136
mighty works, 128
minister
    as biblical preacher, 71-87
    as biblical scholar, 58-70
    as middleman, 59-60
miracle: preaching on the feeding of
    the five thousand
    aims, 137
    brainstorming, 138-44
    context, 132-33
    dynamics, 137-38
    exegesis, 133-36
    names, 145
    outline, 144
    personal involvement, 136
    propositions, 137
    text, 131
miracles, 126-45
    allegorical touches, 135
    avoided, 126-27
    biblical names for, 127-28
    books about, 130
    clue in parables, 130
    clusterings in scripture, 129-30
    interpreting, 127-31
    and law, 131
    seen by faith, 128
    as test of faith, 127
*Modern Use of the Bible, The* (Fos-
    dick), 131
Molech, 184

motto text, 154-56
myth: *see* perplexing passage
Nahum, 49
Nathan's parable, 108-10
*Nature, Man and God* (Temple), 126
*Neurotic Personality of Our Times,
    The* (Horney), 102
new birth, 29-30
new creation (new birth, resurrec-
    tion), 29-30
*New Hermeneutic, The* (Robinson
    and Cobb), 36
*New Look in Preaching, A* (Pike),
    201-5
Nixon, Leroy, 39

Obadiah, 49
"Omega Point," 141, 143
*Out of My Life and Thought*
    (Schweitzer), 80
outlines
    feeding the five thousand, 144
    Jacob, 104-6
    parable of the talents, 123-25
    psalm 139, 176-77
    testing of Abraham, 191-93

Paddan-Aram, 100
"Panegyric on Abraham" (Kierke-
    gaard), 189-90
parable of the talents, preaching on
    aim, 121
    brainstorming, 121-23
    context, 115-17
    exegesis, 117-19
    key verse, 121
    names, 125
    outlines, 123-25
    personal involvement, 119-20
    proposition, 121
    text, 114
parables of Jesus
    books about, 112n
    laborers in the vineyard, 111
    sons of the bridechamber, 111-12
    structure of, 112-13
    the talents, 115-25
    unjust steward, 112

221

parables, preaching on
  allegorizing, 111
  guiding principles, 113-14
  moralizing, 111-12
parallelism, Hebrew poetry, 162-63
Passover, 133, 136
Paul VI, Pope, 22
Peace Corps, 140
pendulum, law of, 80
Pentecost, 48
periscopes, 147
perplexing passage, preaching on
  aim, 188
  brainstorming, 188-91
  context, 182-84
  exegesis, 184-86
  key verses, 188
  names, 193
  outlines, 191-93
  personal involvement, 186-88
  proposition, 188
  text, 181
Phenomenon of Man, The (Teilhard
  de Chardin), 142
Pike, James A., 201-5
Pilate, 128-29
planned preaching, 62-63
Plato, 168
poetry, Hebrew, 162-64
positive and moral commands, 19
précis, 70
  on Jacob, 100-102
  on psalm 139, 173-74
Preaching and Congregation (von Allmen), 73, 194-95
Preaching of the Gospel, The (Barth),
  194-95
Preaching on the Books of the New
  Testament (Stevenson), 62
Preaching on the Books of the Old
  Testament (Stevenson), 44, 62
preparation, 76, 78-79, 86
pre-existence of Christ, 40
prodigal son, 14, 15
proof text, 157
psalm, interpreting a, 159-64
psalm 139, preaching on, 159-77
  aim, 172

psalm—cont'd
  brainstorming, 174-75
  context, 165
  dynamics, 172-73
  exegesis, 165-70
  outlines, 176-77
  personal involvement, 171-72
  précis, 173-74
  proposition, 172
  text, 164-65

Rachel, 100-101
Rambo, Victor, 140
ransom (redemption), 26-27
rationalization, 202
Reaching People from the Pulpit
  (Stevenson and Diehl), 81
"Reaping More Than We Sow," 205-9
reconciliation, 31
redeeming the firstborn, 184
redemption, 55
redemptive Word, 40-41, 42
renunciation, 76, 79
repression, 202
Republic, The (Plato), 168
resurrection, 29-30, 128
reverence for life, 80
Richardson, Robert, 21
River Jordan, The (Glueck), 104
Russo, François, 22

sacrificial system, 27-29
salvation, 25-33
  analogies of: blood atonement, 27-
    29; growing into maturity, 32;
    healing, 30-31; new creation, 29-30;
    ransom, 26-27; reconciliation, 31
Samuel, 49, 179
schedule of study and preparation, 81-
  83
Schweitzer, Albert, 80
Second Advent, 20, 120
self-acceptance, 202
self-criticism, 202
"Sense of Belonging, The" (sermon),
  83
sermon
  delivery, 81

sermon—*cont'd*
grown, not manufactured, 75-87
manuscript, 81
organizing too early, 60
planning for a year, 62-63
pseudo-biblical, 71-75
tape recording, 81
teaching through, 195-96
weekly schedule, 81-83
*Shaking of the Foundations, The* (Tillich), 166
Shakespeare, 155, 209
signs, 127-28
Smythe, Lewis, 139
social salvation, 25
Sockman, Ralph W., 72
Sodomites of Gibeah, 179
Stevenson, Robert Louis, 209
storm on Lake Galilee, 132, 133
strophic structure, Hebrew poetry, 163-64
*Systematic Theology* (Tillich), 41

Teilhard de Chardin, 142-43
Temple, William, 126
Terrien, Samuel, 170
testing of Abraham, 181-93
text
choice of, 61-63
dynamics, 69-70
ending with, 201
exegesis of, 64-66
internal unity, 68-69
longer texts, 61-62
personal involvement, 67-68
placed in context, 63-64
précis, 70
short texts: choice of, 148-53; developing, 153-58; origin, 146; use of, 147

textual preaching, 61-70, 147-58
thematic preaching: *see* doctrinal sermons
Tillich, Paul, 31, 40-41, 48, 103, 166
topical preaching, 14, 55
Torah, 181
Toynbee, Arnold, 123
Turner, Nancy Byrd, 191

"understanding distance, the," 212, 213
urban renewal, 139
*Urgency of Preaching, The* (Haselden), 150-52
Uriah, 108

verification, 78, 80-81
von Allmen, Jean-Jacques, 73, 128, 194-95
von Rad, Gerhard, 186

Whittingham, William, 146
wonders, 127-28
*Word and Faith* (Ebeling), 52
Word of God
according to Calvin, 38
according to Luther, 39-40
according to Tillich, 40-41
as acts of God, 37, 42, 43
and the Bible, 17, 37-38
and conscience, 51
and hermeneutic, 36
inaudible language, 34-35
as personal word tc individuals, 44, 56
as saving life of covenant community, 43
superior to deed, 35-36
through preaching, 40
translated into verb, 212